OUTDOOR LIFE

THE NATURAL DISASTER SURVIVAL HANDBOOK

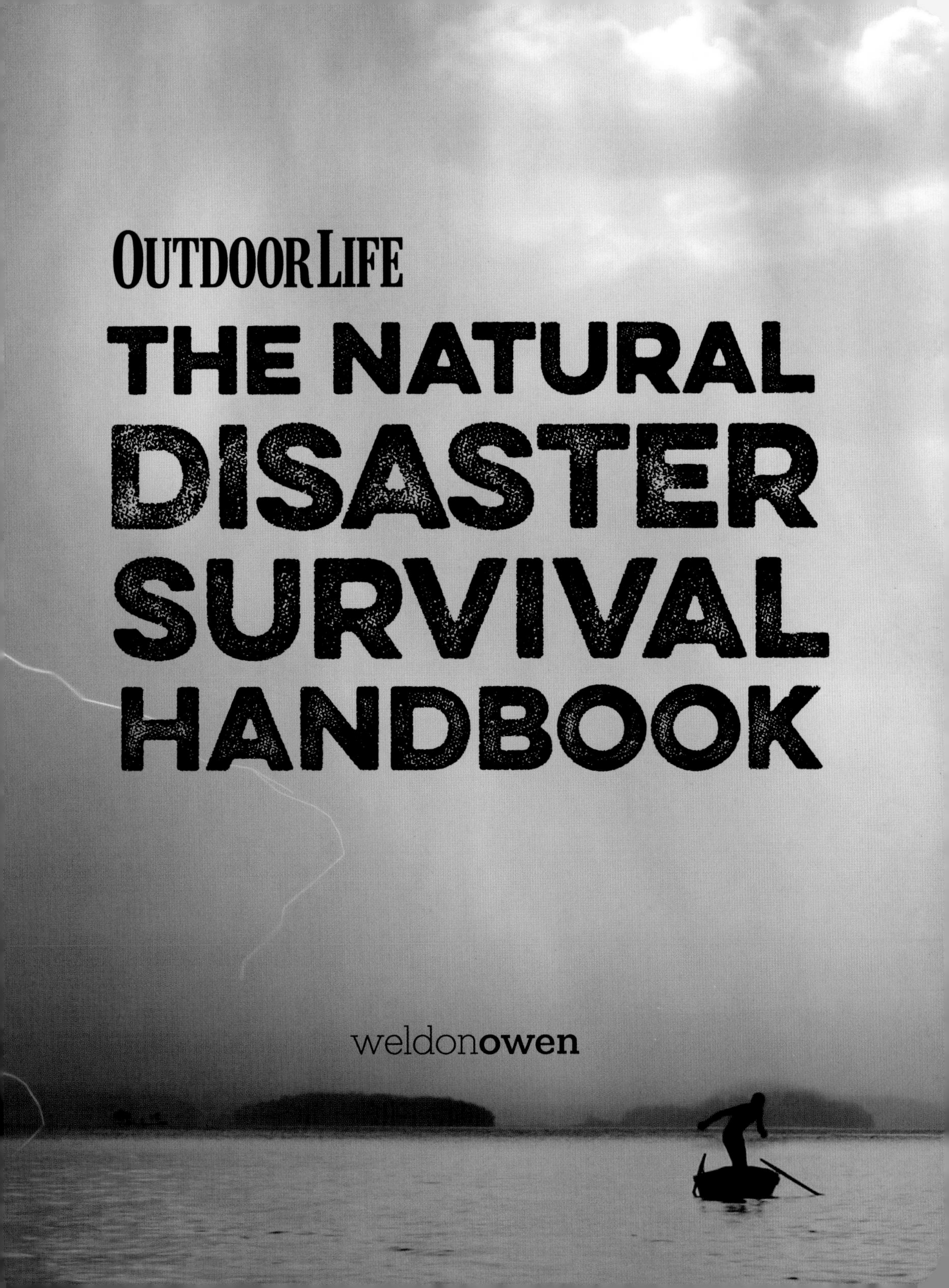

OUTDOOR LIFE

THE NATURAL DISASTER SURVIVAL HANDBOOK

weldon**owen**

CONTENTS

BASICS

COLD & WET

HIGH WIND ADVISORY

ON SHAKY GROUND

CONTENTS

HOT & BOTHERED

DISASTERS ARE GREAT EQUALIZERS.

They strike the rich and the poor, the sick and the healthy, the young and the old alike. But those who are wise enough to prepare or clever enough to adapt to whatever comes their way—be it blizzards and ice, hurricanes and tornadoes, earthquakes or volcanic eruptions, or heat waves and raging wildfires—will survive and thrive. You know these people: They're the ones with a stockpile of water and nonperishable food and a battery-powered radio in their homes and an ICE (in case of emergency) card in their wallets. This book is your ticket to join these resilient ranks— to leave and breathe easier each day knowing you can handle almost any situation life throws at you. There's no time like the present to be prepared for the future.

DISASTER BASICS

ARE YOU PREPARED FOR THE WORST?

Natural disasters may feel like they belong in the realm of Hollywood movies or like something that seems to happen to someone else. After all, it can be uncomfortable to think about circumstances where things might be out of your control and the outcome is uncertain. But the fact is emergency situations can happen to anyone. This book isn't intended to scare you with worst-case scenarios. It's intended for everyday people who want to be more informed and prepared, no matter what life brings. Your willingness to increase your awareness, take steps to plan ahead, and accept that life sometimes means handling tough situations with as much calm determination you can manifest will help you be resilient and prevail.

1 AVOID A WORLD OF TROUBLE

This map shows where in the world some of the most common natural disasters occur.

VOLCANOES Activity occurs largely around the Ring of Fire, the Pacific region that includes Hawaii and Japan. A second active area extends from Java all the way through the Himalayas and the Mediterranean.

EARTHQUAKES Most commonly occurring along the edge of the earth's tectonic plates— sublayers of the earth that float and move—

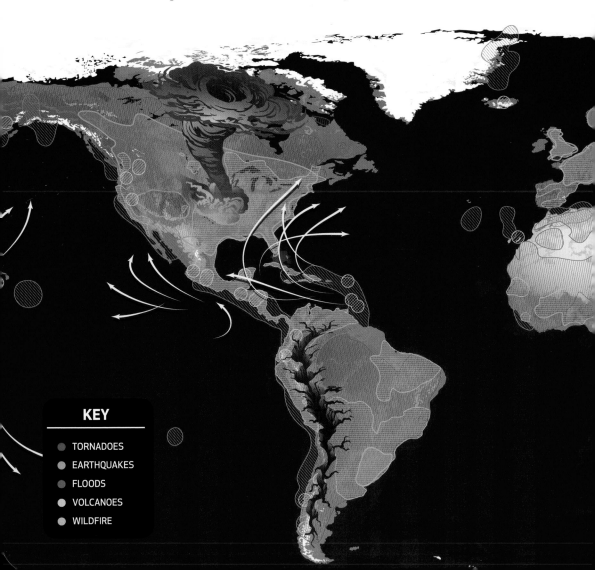

KEY

- TORNADOES
- EARTHQUAKES
- FLOODS
- VOLCANOES
- WILDFIRE

quakes also can be caused by volcanic activity, landslides, mining, fracking, and drilling.

HURRICANES Also known as cyclones or typhoons, these storms range widely as they are propelled by massively powerful winds.

FLOODS While flooding can be caused by a number of factors, including dams failing or dikes being breached, in the natural world, flooding follows seasonal snowmelt and storms, and they can occur anywhere rain falls heavily.

WILDFIRES Not only triggered by lightning or human error, wildfires are becoming more common around the world as the climate changes and more frequent periods of drought and dry seasons increase fire risk.

TORNADOES Tornadoes happen when the right confluence of thunderstorms and complex air patterns come together. They devastate the central and southern United States and are common in Europe and Australia as well.

2 CHART YOUR PRIORITIES

Knowing how to prioritize for a given disaster is important so you don't end up focusing on the wrong thing and wasting what time you may have to prepare for your own safety. Start with the first priority and work down the list. Circumstances may change quickly; be prepared to adapt to changing conditions.

	PRIORITY 1	PRIORITY 2	PRIORITY 3	PRIORITY 4	PRIORITY 5
TSUNAMI	If imminent, get to high ground immediately.	Check Internet, weather radio, or broadcast media for news in your area.	Prepare to evacuate; gather supplies and go bags.	Secure your home; move valuable items to the highest floor.	Shut off utilities.
EARTHQUAKE	Get to a safe place: Drop, cover, and hold on!	Stay there until it's safe, or leave if it's too dangerous to stay.	Shut off utilities after the quake.	Seek shelter if your home is no longer safe.	Inventory supplies.
FLOODING	Check Internet, weather radio, or broadcast media for news in your area.	Prepare to evacuate; gather supplies and go bags.	Learn the safe evacuation route if needed.	Secure and sandbag your home.	Consider proactively evacuating.
TORNADO		Seek cover in a shelter or an interior windowless room.	Await the all-clear signal via siren, Internet, or news.	Assess if your area is still at risk.	Evacuate to another shelter if yours is no longer sound.
HURRICANE		If time allows, board up windows; sandbag and secure your home.	Gather supplies and go bags.	Decide whether to shelter in place or evacuate.	If evacuating, shut off utilities before leaving.
VOLCANO		Decide whether to shelter in place or evacuate.		Wear goggles and dust masks to protect your eyes and airway.	Seal doors, windows, and ducts against ash; turn off fans and air conditioners.
WILDFIRES		Fill up the gas tank in the vehicle intended for evacuation.		Shut off gas main; turn off propane tanks.	Consider proactively evacuating.
POWER FAILURE		Activate solar chargers or prepare portable emergency generators.		Inventory supplies.	Ration battery-powered devices to maximize operational life.

3 CREATE YOUR FAMILY EMERGENCY PLAN

In the event of an emergency, a well-thought-out—and often-drilled—family emergency plan can eliminate stress, limit confusion, and save a great deal of wasted time. Instead of wondering what to do or when to do it, you can put your emergency plan to work right away, bringing sanity, calm and safety to dangerous situations.

Your emergency plan should include the following:

- Up-to-date contact information cards or sheets for each family member

- Communication strategies to keep in touch with options in case the phones are out

- Self-sufficiency skills and supplies, should you have to shelter in place without utilities

- Evacuation plans and routes, should you have to leave your home

- A plan and supplies for the care of pets and livestock

- The knowledge and tools to shut off your utilities

- Ways to assist or care for family who have mobility or medical issues, communication difficulties, or special needs

- Specialized supplies for any infants, young children, or elderly members of your family

- Learning and practicing safety skills, such as first aid, CPR, and fire prevention

- The maintenance, inspection, and rotation of emergency supplies, such as nonperishable food, water, first aid, lighting, and communication equipment

4 CONDUCT DRILLS

Mark some dates on your calendar to perform emergency drills with your family. They may not want to participate, but find a way to get them involved nevertheless. Here are some emergency drills that can keep a family's skills sharp.

DISTANT CONTACT Have each family member contact a friend or family member who lives outside your area—without using a phone (cell or landline). This could be done through e-mail, social media, satellite phone, ham radio, or even a carrier pigeon. Get creative!

SUPPLY SHAKEDOWN Pull out all your emergency supplies, take inventory, check expiration dates, use up older items, replace them with new supplies, and make sure you end up with a few more items than you started with.

FIRE DRILL For starters, perform a classic fire drill, evacuating the home at an unexpected time. Make sure you have a planned meeting spot outside the home, and have everyone low-crawl out of the house. For more practiced families, eliminate the easy exits and add some obstacles. Also, round out the exercise with some stop, drop, and roll each time you have a fire drill.

EVAC Take the fire drill exercise one step further with a mock evacuation. Tell everyone that they have two minutes to grab some clothes and supplies and get to the family vehicle.

5 KEEP IN CONTACT

It's important that everyone in your household knows the plan for getting in touch with everyone else after a disaster. Even if you've loaded all the information into your mobile phones, consider also keeping a paper copy in case your phone is dead when you need the information.

Include contact information for each member of your household with full name, relation to the family, work and/or school address and phone, mobile phone, e-mail, and any other info that might be relevant.

Don't forget to include additional important information, such as date of birth, medical insurance policy numbers and phone numbers, blood type, allergies, or medical conditions. Also add names and contact information for any designated out-of-town family contacts.

List muster or evacuation points from your family plan. Review and update the information in the plan annually. Additionally, ensure all members of your household have ICE entries (see item 7).

ᴳ COMMUNICATE IN A DISASTER

During a regional emergency or disaster, mobile phone systems very quickly become overloaded with voice calls. If you cannot get through, try text messaging instead, as that has a much higher chance of getting through during these types of circumstances.

If you want to communicate to everyone easily with a single step, consider posting to Twitter, Facebook, or other social media with your status. Alternatively, the Red Cross offers a free Safe and Well online listing service. Just be sure to plan with other members of your household which of these systems you'll use should you not be reachable by phone.

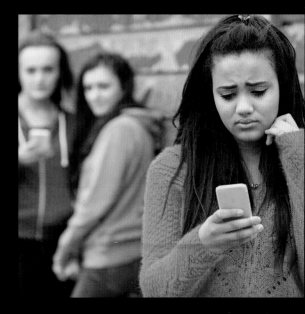

7

BE AWARE OF ICE

In case of emergency, or ICE, is a concept that came about in 2005 when it became apparent that mobile phones were ubiquitous and were a great way to inform doctors and emergency responders whom to contact in a crisis, simply by programming extra address book entries into their cell phone, such as "ICE, dad" or "ICE, wife."

These days, assuming that you are carrying a smartphone, it's a little more complicated since your screen is probably locked. However, both Android and iOS phones are able to show a list of designated emergency contacts from the lock screen if you choose to make them visible to others.

Other options include putting a sticker on the back of your phone or ID with your contacts. Or print out an ICE card for your wallet, purse, or glove compartment (see item 8, next page).

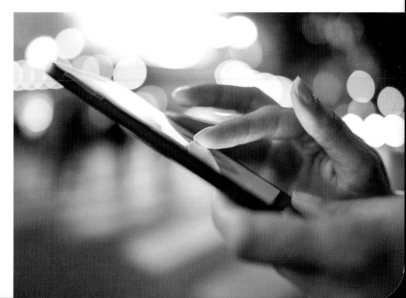

8 CARRY A CARD

Many insurance companies and automobile associations offer free versions of an ICE card that you can download and carry in your wallet or glove box. Or you can photocopy or scan and fill out the one provided here to make things easier for first responders and for you and your loved ones in case of an emergency.

ICE *In Case of Emergency*

OUTDOOR LIFE

VEHICLE DRIVERS

PRIMARY (FULL NAME): _____

SECONDARY (FULL NAME): _____

ICE CONTACTS

PHYSICIAN: _____ ALLERGIES: _____

MEDICAL CONDITIONS: _____

NAME/RELATION: _____

PHONE 1: _____ PHONE 2: _____

NAME/RELATION: _____

PHONE 1: _____ PHONE2: _____

NAME/RELATION: _____

PHONE 1: _____ PHONE2: _____

ICE *In Case of Emergency*

NAME

ICE CONTACTS

PHYSICIAN: _____

ALLERGIES: _____

MEDICAL CONDITIONS: _____

NAME/RELATION: _____

PHONE 1: _____

PHONE 2: _____

NAME/RELATION: _____

PHONE 1: _____

PHONE2: _____

NAME/RELATION: _____

PHONE 1: _____

PHONE2: _____

9 UNDERSTAND THE CRISIS

Being prepared for disaster means knowing the possibilities. Sometimes, a full-blown state of emergency is just a more extreme version of the minor inconveniences you've faced once (or many times) before.

LEVEL 1	LEVEL 2	LEVEL 3	LEVEL 4
Power outage	Rolling brownouts	Weeklong blackout	Grid failure
Aftershocks	Minor quakes	Major quakes	The Big One
Volcanic ash interferes with air travel	Heat and ash cause health issues	Evacuations/ local destruction of cities	Megavolcanic eruption

10 GET FAMILIAR WITH SCOPE

With all these potential disasters, you may be wondering where to start. Let's look at the reach of each type of crisis.

MINOR, SMALL-SCOPE DISASTER	Local area	A few hours to a few days	Limited services and utilities; available food and water; intact national infrastructure
MINOR, LARGE-SCOPE DISASTER	Regional area	5–14 days	Limited services and utilities; limited amounts of food, water, and fuel; intact national infrastructure
MAJOR DISASTER	National area	15–60 days	No services and utilities; no food, water, or fuel; some disruption of national infrastructure
GLOBAL DISASTER	Worldwide	More than two months	No services and utilities; no food, water, or fuel; complete collapse of government and/or financial infrastructures

11 PACK A BOB FOR ANY SITUATION

A bug-out bag (BOB) is a collection of goods that you would need to survive if you had to flee your home with no guarantee of shelter, food, or water during an emergency. Think of the BOB as your survival insurance policy for any disaster or mayhem. There may not be one perfect, universally agreed-upon set of equipment, but with a good core set of items (similar to those used in backpacking), you can put together a BOB suited for a wide variety of situations. Most people use either a backpack or a duffel bag as a container for their goods,

which should include basic survival essentials and a few irreplaceable items. Fill up your BOB with a minimum of the things listed in the black box with most items sealed in ziplock bags to prevent damage.

Keep your main BOB safe and ready to go in a secure location with modified versions in your car and office. It's also a good idea for you to have "everyday carry" (EDC) items— survival essentials that you can carry in your pocket or purse. Here's a breakdown for these different types of kits:

- Shelter items like a small tent and sleeping bag or a tarp and blanket
- A couple quarts (or liters) of drinking water, and purification equipment to disinfect more water
- High-calorie, no-cook foods like protein bars, peanut butter, trail mix, etc.
- First-aid, sanitation, and hygiene supplies
- Several fire-starting devices
- A small pot for boiling water or cooking
- A few basic tools like a knife, duct tape, rope, etc.
- Extra clothes appropriate for the season
- Flashlight with extra batteries
- Cash
- A digital backup of all your important documents and artifacts. This could be a thumb drive with your bank information, insurance documents, wills, and family photos and videos

ITEM	HOME /CAR	OFFICE	EDC
High-calorie, no-cook foods	●	●	
Bottled water	●	●	
Tent or tarp	●		
Sleeping bag	●		
Lighter or fire-starting gear	●		●
Change of rugged clothing	●	●	
Flashlight & extra batteries	●	●	●
Pocket knife	●	●	●
Can opener	●		
Heavy cord	●		
Battery-operated radio	●		
Battery-op or solar/crank cell-phone charger	●		
First aid kit	●		
Sanitation items	●		
Meds, eyeglasses, hearing aid batteries, etc.	●		
Snare wire	●		
Signal mirror	●		●
Whistle	●	●	●
Change of shoes & socks	●	●	
Small pen & paper	●		
Duct tape	●		
Razor blades	●		
Water filter	●		
Water purification tablets	●		
Adhesive bandages	●	●	
Disinfectant wipes	●		
Fishing kit	●		
Bouillon cubes	●		
Tinfoil	●		
Small shovel	●		
Snow chains or a sand bag	●		
Car-safety items, including jumper cables, flares, reflective sign, tow strap, ice scraper	●		

12 STOCK YOUR HOME

Chances are, we've all experienced a power outage at one point or another. Usually, it's in the middle of our favorite television program or movie, and the response is one of disappointment, sometimes profane, at the interruption. The reality, however, is that most households are unprepared for losing that power for anything longer than a couple of hours. What happens if, on top of no power, the water also runs out? What are you going to do when the freezer thaws out after 24 hours without electricity? What if you have special medical needs? Are you prepared? Home survival isn't that different from wilderness survival. The benefit is that you don't have to carry everything you'll need. And you also can benefit from some household hacks to turn run-of-the-mill products into life-saving materials:

❶ **WATER** Have a weeks' worth for you and your family (one gallon per person per day—and don't forget about pets!). If bottled water runs out, remember there's water in the tanks of your toilets. If you're lucky and you have advance notice that your water supply might be jeopardized, fill up your bathtub with water so you have extra.

❷ **FOOD** You can survive a surprisingly long time without food, so food is less of a concern. Stock up on easy dried foods to get you through the worst of it. Canned foods that don't need heating are a good idea, as are prepackaged, high-calorie snacks. Rather than storing rice and beans in their original bags, which can rip, transfer them into 2-liter bottles for easy storing.

③ MEDICAL SUPPLIES When you're making your at-home medical kit, think big. Spend time and a little extra cash to cover all the potential medical issues you might encounter. You also should prepare to deal with your prescription medical needs. Some medications—insulin, for example—need to be kept refrigerated.

④ RADIO A battery-powered radio is sufficient for a few days if you need to monitor emergency services (be sure you have a good supply the correct batteries on hand or it's no use at all! In the U.S., look for a model that includes NOAA weather bands. A hand-powered radio is even better for your emergency kit. Current models also include cell-phone chargers—a potential life-saver.

⑤ CANDLES AND MATCHES If you're out of candles, raid the kids' rooms for crayons. A single crayon will burn for half an hour. Or you can put a wick in a can of vegetable shortening for a long-lasting candle.

⑥ DUCT TAPE You can do virtually anything with it. Really.

⑦ SHELTER AND WARMTH Chances are, you already have enough blankets in your house to help keep your family warm. But it's never a bad idea to have some survival blankets as part of your emergency preparedness kit. It's also a good idea to keep some rain tarps handy, just in case you end up with a hole in your roof or some other damage to your home that ends up exposing you to the elements.

13 MITIGATE HOME DISASTER

Use this easy reference guide to check off the various things you can do to reduce the risk or severity of the problems you're likely to encounter in the event of the most common natural disasters.

KEY

- BASIC SAFETY
- EARTHQUAKE
- FLOODING
- HIGH WINDS
- FIRE
- FREEZING

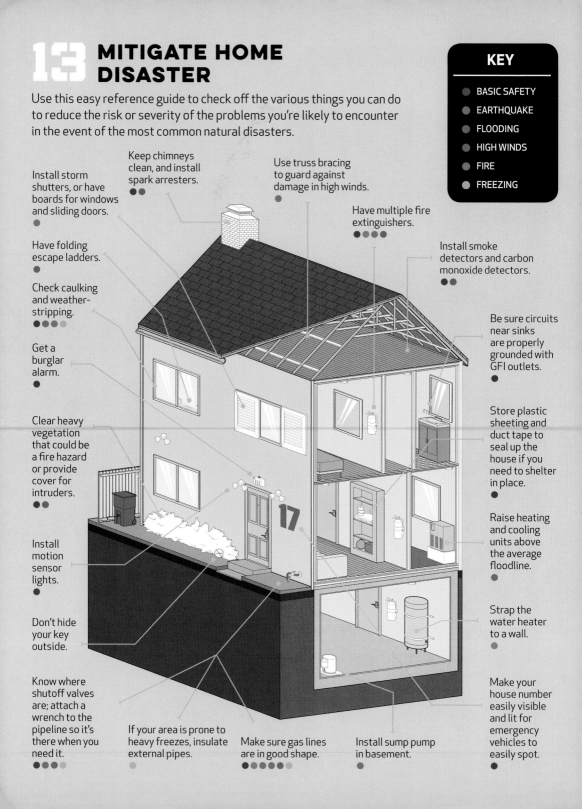

Keep chimneys clean, and install spark arresters.

Install storm shutters, or have boards for windows and sliding doors.

Use truss bracing to guard against damage in high winds.

Have multiple fire extinguishers.

Install smoke detectors and carbon monoxide detectors.

Have folding escape ladders.

Check caulking and weather-stripping.

Be sure circuits near sinks are properly grounded with GFI outlets.

Get a burglar alarm.

Store plastic sheeting and duct tape to seal up the house if you need to shelter in place.

Clear heavy vegetation that could be a fire hazard or provide cover for intruders.

Raise heating and cooling units above the average floodline.

Install motion sensor lights.

Strap the water heater to a wall.

Don't hide your key outside.

Know where shutoff valves are; attach a wrench to the pipeline so it's there when you need it.

If your area is prone to heavy freezes, insulate external pipes.

Make sure gas lines are in good shape.

Install sump pump in basement.

Make your house number easily visible and lit for emergency vehicles to easily spot.

17

14
MAKE IT THROUGH A POWER OUTAGE

A power outage suddenly reduces your stovetop to mere counter space and makes your refrigerator no better for food storage than a pantry. But you've still got to eat.

MIND THE EXPIRATION DATE Open the refrigerator door only when necessary to keep perishables and frozen food fresh. Usually food in the fridge is edible for a day, and food in the freezer for a couple of days.

IMPROVISE A FRIDGE If it looks as if the power outage is going to last a few days or (gulp) a few weeks, you can store your perishable foods in camp coolers or on blocks of ice in the bathtub.

COOK SAFELY Never fire up a BBQ or a hibachi or start an open fire in the house. Instead, cook outdoors on a propane grill or use a Dutch oven and briquettes. If your fireplace is equipped with an iron-top inset, you can cook on that.

APPLY THE SNIFF TEST Discard unsafe foods that have a foul odor, color, or texture. Even when you're hungry, fuzz growing on the food is a bad sign.

15
KEEP IT TOGETHER

If you keep your camping gear down in the basement, your disaster supplies in a closet, and your tools in your garage, you're not unusual—but you're also at a disadvantage in an emergency. Instead, store your tools and camping gear with your disaster supplies. You can easily grab items as you need them for, say, a camping trip or DIY project, but you won't have to scramble for essentials in an emergency, especially if your home is partially destroyed or inaccessible. Consider buying some large sturdy plastic storage tubs, keep everything labeled and organized, and don't forget to return anything you borrow from your stash. If you need to evacuate quickly, just grab the tubs and go.

COLD'S WET TEARS

BAD WEATHER? YOU'RE SOAKING IN IT.

Rain and snow are essential to our very survival—and yet, they can also mean disaster. Heavy snow grounds airplanes, knocks out power lines, and makes the roads a nightmare for anyone caught unawares. And even when it isn't snowing, cold winter weather can be a deadly threat whether you're stuck in a car or huddled under a blanket at home wondering when the heat is going to come back on. Once the weather warms, it's time for thunderstorms, snowmelt, and flooding. In other words, unless you live in the most arid of desert conditions, you'll likely have to worry about water in some form some day, whether it's frozen, pelting from the sky, or rising ominously in your basement. Want to stay warm and dry? Read on.

KNOW WHAT'S FALLING ON YOU

	WINTER RAIN	SNOW	SLEET	FREEZING RAIN	GRAUPEL	FREEZING FOG
PRECIPITATION TYPE						
CONDITIONS FOR FORMATION	Most wintertime rain in cold climates forms when snow falls into above-freezing air and completely melts before reaching the ground.	Snow forms when the right mixture of moisture, cold air, and lift come together in the atmosphere. May also result from children wearing pajamas inside-out.	Sleet forms when a snowflake partially melts and refreezes into an ice pellet before reaching the ground.	Snowflakes melt in a layer of above-freezing air; the droplets fall into subfreezing air at the surface and freeze on contact.	Graupel forms when water vapor deposits ice on snowflakes.	Fog that develops when air temperatures are below freezing.
APPEARANCE	Small, cold liquid droplets that sting like ice, because they were ice a few minutes ago.	Snow can range from tiny, powdery flakes to huge, terrifying globs that land with a thud.	Small, white ice pellets that bounce and tink when they hit exposed surfaces.	It looks just like rain, but it leaves an icy glaze on any exposed surface.	Graupel has the look and feel of Dippin' Dots™. It tinks like sleet but falls apart like snow.	Freezing fog can be deceiving because it looks like regular fog, but it's far more dangerous.
ASSOCIATED RISKS	Wet roads and potential flooding.	Slick roads, joyful students, rooftop and tree damage, and dangerously reduced visibility.	Sleet accumulates like snow, but it tends to freeze into a thick sheet of ice before you can remove it.	Icy roads and sidewalks, tree damage, prolonged power outages.	Graupel has the same impacts and risks as snow.	Reduced visibility, a thin glaze of ice on exposed surfaces, accumulating ice in some conditions.

17 UNDERSTAND WINDCHILL

You don't need a weatherman to know which way the wind blows, but you might want to listen to him when he tells you that it'll be windy when it's bitterly cold.

CHILLY AIR An air temperature of 0°F (-18°C) is cold enough, but when you factor in a 25 mph (40 km/h) wind, the weather is downright unbearable unless you're wrapped up from head to toe. One common measure we use during the winter is the windchill, or how cold the combination of frigid temperatures and stiff winds feels on exposed skin.

LOSING THE BUBBLE On a calm, cold morning, your skin is partially protected by a bubble of warmth radiating from your body. When the wind starts blowing, it can remove this layer of warm air, exposing your skin directly to the elements. The cold, dry wind accelerates your body's heat loss by evaporating

moisture from your skin, causing your surface temperature to further plummet.

FREEZING COLD If the air is cold enough, your skin can begin to freeze, leading to a serious medical condition called frostbite. The effects of frostbite can range from mild redness and a burning and stinging sensation to complete skin cell death, which requires expert intervention (and in the most extreme cases, may even need amputation).

CHART IT OUT The National Weather Service uses a formula developed by scientists to determine windchill. Using this formula, it's pretty easy to tell what the windchill will be. In the "Chilly Air" example above left, a temperature of 0°F (-18°C) and a 25 mph (40 km/h) wind would produce a dangerous windchill of -24°F (-31°C); frostbite would develop in just 30 minutes of exposure to those conditions.

183 PREPARE FOR A NOR'EASTER

Nor'easters are a snow-lover's dream, but they can quickly turn into a nightmare for the amount of damage and trouble they can produce. Here's a look at the different impacts you can expect during one of these severe winter storms.

RISK LEVEL	WHAT TO EXPECT	HOW TO PREPARE
HEAVY SNOW — VERY HIGH	Deep accumulations of heavy, wet snow. Impassible roads, tree and roof damage, and unmanageable drifts are possible.	Proactively trim trees and clear snow from your roof to prevent damage. Exercise regularly to reduce risk of injury while shoveling. If you can't handle shoveling, get someone else to do it!
DAMAGING WINDS — HIGH	The strong pressure gradient in nor'easters results in winds that can reach hurricane force.	Secure or bring inside loose items that could blow around and cause damage. Prepare for extended power outages as a precaution.
BEACH EROSION — HIGH	Strong winds, waves, and flooding can cause beach erosion. Homes right on the coast can sustain damage (or even get destroyed) by the coast falling into the ocean.	Do your part to keep sand dunes, vegetation, and fences intact so sand builds up and remains on the beaches. If you're right on the coast, prepare to evacuate if things get dicey.
HEAVY RAIN — MEDIUM	When the atmosphere is a little too warm for snow, nor'easters can produce heavy rainfall. A couple of inches (5 cm) of rain are possible.	Rain is harmless unless it falls too heavily for storm drains to handle. Rain falling on snowpack can cause localized flooding and building damage.
FREEZING RAIN — MEDIUM	Ice accretion from freezing rain is possible in that transition zone between regular rain and snow. On rare occasions, significant ice storms can result from nor'easters.	Keep rock salt, sand, and cat litter on hand to help melt ice and provide traction to walk and drive. Also have plenty of food, water, medicine, and cash in case your power goes out.
STORM SURGE — MEDIUM	Strong winds coinciding with high tide can cause a storm surge (push water ashore), as in a minimal hurricane.	Take precautions to prevent flood damage, and evacuate if told to do so by local authorities.

19

RIDE OUT A BLIZZARD AT HOME

Once a blizzard hits, all you can do is sit tight; there's no skipping out to the grocery store for supplies when visibility is zero. Get your act together while the clouds are still gathering.

STOCK UP Make sure your at-home survival kit is well loaded with the usual essentials, plus extra blankets, sleeping bags, and heavy coats and other warm clothing.

STAY WARM A storm might tear down power lines, and without electricity you can't operate a furnace. So get a generator or stock up on fuel for a wood-burning stove or fireplace. And if you're not on your own, huddle with others in a small room to combine and maximize body heat. It's not pervy: It's survival.

WATCH YOUR WATER Severe cold can freeze pipes, leaving you without water to drink or the ability to flush a toilet more than one last time. Store water in containers where it won't freeze.

REDECORATE STRATEGICALLY Hang quilts over windows for extra insulation. In the daytime, keep your curtains and blinds open to allow sunlight to warm up your home. At night, keep them shut to trap heat inside.

20 SHUT DOWN A HOME FOR WINTER

A lot can go wrong in a home that's left empty in the winter, whether for months or just a week or two. To avoid returning to a big mess—or worse—take these basic steps. When getting a summer home ready to stand empty all winter, take the time to work through all of these steps as appropriate. If you need to evacuate your home in an emergency you may not have the time to complete all of the tasks described here. If you need to work fast, shut down the water and electricity first, then handle the rest as time allows.

FRIDGE Unplug the fridge, and empty all of the contents. Bring them with you, and prop the fridge and freezer doors open to prevent mold.

CABINETS OR PANTRY Bring any canned and jarred foods with you, as these containers will likely burst if their contents freeze. Dry goods such as flour, sugar, cereals, rice, and the like, may be left behind, as they are not usually harmed by the cold; place them in metal containers to prevent rodents from having a party while you're gone.

WATER PIPE Turn off the water at the outside meter if you're on municipal water, or turn off your pump and empty the pressure tank if you're in a rural area with a well. Once turned off, open every faucet and valve in the home to drain all of the lines.

WATER HEATER Drain the water heater. Make sure you turn off the power first, if it's an electric unit, otherwise you'll burn up the heating elements.

TOILET TANK Once the house's water supply has been turned off, flush the toilet to empty the tank. Any water that's still left in the tank can be sopped up with a towel or mixed with a splash of antifreeze to prevent freeze damage.

TOILET BOWL After turning off the water and draining the lines and toilet tank, pour 1 liter (or quart) of rubbing alcohol or vehicle engine antifreeze into the bowl. This will prevent the water from freezing—which can break the toilet in half.

SINKS AND SHOWERS All sinks and showers will need the same antifreeze treatment as the toilet. Pour half a liter (or quart) of antifreeze in each drain right before leaving after you have used the fixture for the last time.

GAS METER Turn off any propane or LP gas that supplies the home. After your return, make sure a professional turns the gas back on and checks all gas systems before you occupy the home again.

RAT TRAP Place mouse or rat traps around the home to catch any marauding mammals. Set them in places where the liquefying rodent won't damage the flooring.

DOORS AND WINDOWS Secure the doors and windows. Lock up tight with additional latches or locks at back doors and strips of wood in the tracks of any sliders. Ask a trustworthy friend to check on the place during your absence.

21 CLEAR A HEAVY SNOW

Folks who live in snow country know the value of a strong roof. A 1-inch (2.5 cm) layer of snow weighs approximately 5 pounds (2.25 kg) per square foot (.09 sq m)—and that can really add up. Sure, a little bit of snow can help insulate your home, but too much poses a hazard and should be removed.

STEP ONE Use an appropriate shovel with a long handle for hard-to-reach areas. Start by clearing the apex of the roof, which will help you maintain a secure footing, then work toward the edges.

STEP TWO Keep your gutters clear to avoid standing water collecting—it will freeze in the cold, potentially causing structural damage to your home when it does.

STEP THREE Don't forget tree branches, which can be brought down from the weight of the snow and ice; they may land on your home, a vehicle, a loved one, or a stranger passing by who happens to know a lawyer. Clear snow and ice by brushing it off the ends of limbs with a shovel, then work your way back to the trunk.

22

SHOVEL SNOW SAFELY

Every year you hear of folks who have heart attacks while shoveling snow, but even young, healthy folks can injure themselves if they're not careful.

Here are a few tips to make sure that no one has to shovel you out when you attempt this chore.

USE THE RIGHT SHOVEL The best shovel has a curved handle that allows you to hold it comfortably when your knees are bent and your back is very slightly flexed (A). A plastic shovel blade will be lighter than a metal one, thus putting less stress on your back. Grip the handle and shaft of the shovel with your hands at least 12 inches (30.5 cm) apart.

WARM UP This is serious exercise (you can burn about 500 calories an hour shoveling and work a lot of muscles), so take it seriously. Stretch a little before you shovel (B), and don't shovel when your muscles are already cold.

PUSH IT You want to push the snow along (C) rather than lift it. If you do have to lift it, lift just as you would any heavy object: squat and lift with your legs, not your back. A full shovel-load of wet snow can weigh as much as 25 pounds (11 kg)!

23

SET UP A SNOW PANTRY

If you lose power in a winter storm, one thing you don't have to worry about is keeping your perishables stored safely. All you need is a shovel, a footlocker, a cooler, or anything that is enclosed with a door to protect your food from scavengers.

STEP 1 Dig a hole in the snow or pile snow up and around the container to cover it in at least 1 foot (30 cm) of snow.

STEP 2 Place all perishable items into individual plastic bags to reduce odors that might attract animals bent on raiding your supplies.

STEP 3 Place food into the container, close, and cover with snow to further insulate it.

DON'T GET LOST

Finding your way can be a problem in snowy conditions and in featureless terrain. If you're short on navigational equipment but need to journey away from camp or car in snowy conditions, you can use these techniques to blaze your own trail across any landscape.

LEAVE SIGNS As you traverse forests or boulder fields, use something to mark your travel direction on prominent trees and rocks. During emergencies, high impact marking (like chopping arrows into tree bark or chipping rock) may be a necessary method. During lower levels of distress, a simple piece of black charcoal from your campfire can be used to draw arrows or write messages on trees, rocks, and other surfaces. Always make your marks at eye level so they won't be missed (by you or by rescuers!).

STACK IT UP A cone of tall sticks, a pile of rocks, or even a snowman can be placed in open areas to indicate the trail at a distance or to signal other useful information, such as the location of cached supplies. Arrows and other signals made of sticks and stones lying on the ground can be used for pathfinding, but a light snow can cover them easily, leaving you stranded.

FLY THE FLAG Strips of colorful fabric or other material can be used to make excellent trail markers in brushy areas and woodland terrain. Consider carrying plastic survey tape in your pack so you don't have to end up ripping up your nice red flannel shirt! Choose bright unnatural colors like hot pink or Day-Glo™ purple. Hang small strips at eye level, within view of the last marker, to make a clear trail.

25

COME IN FROM THE COLD SAFELY

When you've been out shoveling your way out from under that latest blizzard, a cup of hot chocolate and a roaring fire in the fireplace probably sound like the best things in the world. But it helps to take a few simple precautions to make sure you warm up properly.

Chances are, your extremities like fingers and toes have grown incredibly cold. The best way to warm them up is by surprising your partner with frozen hands on his or her warm skin. All joking aside, though, don't go run your digits under hot water right away. Instead, start with cold water, which still will be warmer than your cold skin. Gradually warm up the water until you're feeling normal again.

On a much larger scale, climbing into a steaming hot shower or sauna can cause dizziness and even unconsciousness in rare cases. So if you have been out and are cold, wet, and in need of a warm-up, strip out of your wet clothes first, and follow the same approach as you did to warm up your hands. Start with colder water first, and gradually increase the heat as your body warms up.

26

WALK IN A WHITEOUT

I have a friend who got lost between his house and barn because the snow was falling so fast that he couldn't see the ground—much less the 100 feet (30 m) between the two structures. He survived getting lost in a whiteout. I hope you're as lucky.

RESPECT THE STORM A whiteout is a horror show. You can't imagine how disorienting it is until you're in one. So only venture out as a last resort—say, if you have to get to emergency gear, clear the hood of your car to keep it visible to rescuers, or help someone who is stranded a short distance away.

TIE YOURSELF TO HOME BASE
One way to keep from getting totally lost in a whiteout is to tie one end of a long rope to your starting point and the other end around your waist. The rope doesn't help you reach your destination, but it will help you get back. (If you know a blizzard is coming and you anticipate needing to travel back and forth between buildings, tie a rope between them before the snow starts.)

PROTECT YOUR FACE Cover your mouth and nose to shield them from the wind and snow. Heck, go ahead and cover your eyes, too, since you're definitely not using them to see, so why subject them to abuse.

27

BUILD A SNOW CAVE

In an emergency, a snow cave can provide warmth and shelter on a frigid night.

STEP 1 Find a spot with deep snow, preferably on a hillside so you can dig straight into deep snow. Start off with a low entrance just large enough for you to crawl inside.

STEP 2 After penetrating about 2 feet (60 cm) into the snow, start carving upward to create a dome 4–5 feet (1¼ – 1½ m) tall and maybe half again as wide.

STEP 3 Against the back wall, shape a sleeping bench 2 feet (60 cm) up from the floor. Poke a small hole in the roof beside the door as an air vent.

STEP 4 Crawl in, cover the entrance with a block of snow, then heat the interior with a single candle.

28

MAKE SNOWSHOES

Got some paracord? Got a knife? How about some trees with thin, springy branches? Then you have all you need to lash together a set of emergency snowshoes. If you don't have these crucial items, go back, read the survival kit item again, and check us when you're ready!

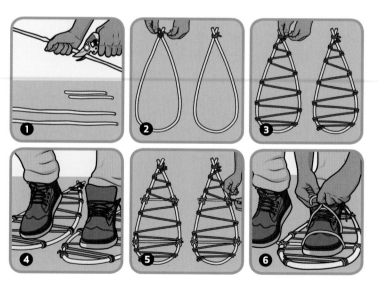

STEP 1 Cut a couple of nice, flexible branches, each at least 3 feet (1 m) in length. Then, cut a couple of small pieces about 6 inches (15 cm) each, and cut a couple measuring about 10 inches (25 cm) long.

STEP 2 Bend each of the long branches into a teardrop shape, and tie it together at the narrow end using paracord.

STEP 3 Lace paracord in a zigzag pattern across the entire length of each shoe.

STEP 4 Test for fit.

STEP 5 Add some bracing crosspieces where your toe and heel will fall using branches.

STEP 6 Tie your boots to the snowshoes.

29 BUILD A FIRE ON SNOW

If you're out in the wilderness unexpectedly (or if the snow was unexpected), you might not be prepared to build a fire in snowy conditions. Here's how to do it.

STEP 1 Use rocks or branches to elevate the fire's base above snow-covered or damp ground. Build your fire on a two-layer fire platform of green, wrist-thick (or larger) branches to raft your blaze above deep snow cover. Lay down a row of 3-foot-long (1 m) branches, then another perpendicular row on top. Stay away from overhanging boughs; rising heat will melt snow trapped in foliage.

STEP 2 Lay out the fuel—and don't scrimp on this step. Collect and organize plenty of dry tinder and kindling and get twice as many large branches as you think you'll need. Super-dry tinder is critical; birch bark, pine needles, wood shavings, pitch splinters, cattail fluff, and the dead, dry twigs from the sheltered lower branches of conifers are standards. Place tinder between your hands and rub vigorously to shred the material. You will need a nest at least as large as a ping-pong ball. Pouring rain and snow? Think creatively: dollar bills, pocket lint, fuzzy wool, and a snipped piece of shirt fabric will work.

STEP 3 Plan the fire so it dries out wet wood as it burns. Place a large branch or dry rock across the back of the fire and arrange wet wood across the fire a few inches above the flame. Don't crisscross; laying the wood parallel will aid the drying process.

30 CROSS ICE CAREFULLY

Crossing a frozen lake or pond is one of the most dangerous outdoor activities. It's especially perilous toward the end of winter, when the ice pack is deteriorating and thickness alone is not an accurate gauge of safety. Here's how to walk on ice safely:

Stay away from inlet and outlet streams. Under-the-ice current can reduce ice strength by 20 percent or more.

Use your walking stick or ice chisel to test ice conditions.

Slushiness is a sign of a weakening pack; so is finding snow cover or water on top of ice. Depressions in the snow indicate a spring.

Tow your equipment sled on a long rope. You can push it toward a victim who has fallen through.

A nice long cord wrapped around an empty plastic jug makes a handy flotation device. Stand on sturdy ice and toss the jug to the victim.

Open water is a red flag, pointing to a marginal ice pack nearer the shore.

Beware of black, gray, or milky ice. It lacks the strength of clear blue or green ice.

Eroded shore ice is a sign of a thinning ice pack. Beware.

Ice sloping from a bank may trap air underneath, reducing its strength.

Pressure ridges are caused by fluctuating temperatures. Avoid them.

Thin cracks may let you see whether the ice is thick or not.

31

SURVIVE A FALL THROUGH ICE

FORGET HYPOTHERMIA The first thing to worry about when you've fallen into ice is getting yourself out. Assuming you have your safety spikes (see item 40), here's what to do.

STEP 1 Turn around in the water so you're facing the way you came. That's probably the strongest ice.

STEP 2 Jam the points of the spikes into the ice.

STEP 3 While kicking your feet vigorously, haul yourself out.

STEP 4 As soon as you're on the ice, roll (don't crawl) away from the edge of the hole. Get off the ice, and get warm immediately.

32

TREAT FROSTBITE

What if you ignored all of our warnings and now you're frostbitten? Your best option is to seek medical help. However, if you're snowbound, here's how to stave off disaster, by which we mean losing your fingers or toes. Never rub frostbitten skin, as you can destroy cells and make it worse.

STEP 1 Get out of the cold. If you'll be continuing to expose your frozen flesh to freezing temperatures, don't treat the frostbite until you've gotten to safety.

STEP 2 Remove any jewelry in case you develop any swelling.

STEP 3 Put the affected area into a bath of body-temperature water. Refresh the water frequently as it cools to keep the water at a steady temperature.

STEP 4 If water isn't available, you can use body heat to treat mild cases of frostbite. You should never position the victim near a heater or an open fire: If there's nerve damage, he or she may not feel tissue begin to burn.

STEP 5 Dress the injury in sterile bandages, wrapping each affected digit individually.

33

PROTECT YOURSELF FROM BITTERLY COLD WINDS

The best way to guard against dangerously cold weather is to make sure that you cover every inch (2.5 cm) of exposed skin before you go outside. Sure, it's uncomfortable to walk around feeling like a marshmallow person or an inept movie criminal because you've got on so many clothes, but it's better to feel and look stupid than lose a chunk of your skin in the name of vanity.

In a perfect world, everyone would have the will to throw on a balaclava, gloves, and a heavy coat before venturing into the frozen tundra (or down to the store), and the money to buy the right gear. Sadly, our world is far from perfect, and it's hard to cover every single bit of your body when it's cold. So, that means many of us will still have to deal with exposed faces as we go about our lives in the frigid air. Standing in a bus shelter or behind a wall will help protect you from the wind, and turning your back to the wind as a last resort is a very useful (and symbolic!) way to stave off your skin's frosty demise.

Don't forget your kids, either. Children are especially vulnerable to cold weather injuries. Many school districts will delay or cancel classes when extreme cold is in the forecast, but some superintendents are determined to make kids risk injury and tough it out like they had to in the old days. If this is the case, make sure your kids are bundled up, and keep an eye on them until they get in the building or on the bus if possible.

34 PREVENT HYPOTHERMIA

Hypothermia is no joke, and it's easy for even a healthy person to fall prey to it while outside during freezing winter weather. A drop in core temperature of just a few degrees can be fatal, and it's likely you won't even see it coming.

One of the first lines of defense your body uses to keep from dying in the extreme cold is to divert blood from the arms and legs to keep it close to the heart and core. This rerouting is exactly why your hands and feet get cold first. Your body then shivers in order to generate heat.

This rarely saves the day. Before long, your muscles will fatigue, and the shivering will cease. This is not a sign that the shivering worked, but rather that the situation is growing more dire as your body shuts down blood circulation to the arms and legs, trying to preserve your vital organs.

Confusion and disorientation set in quickly. To make matters worse, many hypothermia victims feel strangely warm and, in what is called "paradoxical undressing," start stripping off layers of winter clothing, hastening the end. Here's what you can do to avoid this awful fate.

WEAR A HAT You know how your grandma told you that you lose most of your body heat from your head? The truth is you lose heat from whatever's uncovered, which is often your head. So those beanies are more than fashion. At least in winter, they can be lifesavers.

KEEP YOUR COAT ON Wear an appropriate winter coat to keep you warm and dry during cold weather. You want something that is windproof as well as made of wicking fabric, meaning that it pulls moisture away from your body.

CHANGE CLOTHES If you're working outside, you may feel warm from activity. If you're working hard enough to sweat, though, you're actually going to lose heat from the wet fabric of your clothes. Take time every hour or so to go inside and put on dry clothes.

WATCH THE SHIVERING If you're outside in freezing weather and notice that you're starting to feel warmer even though the ambient temperature has remained steady, it's time to go inside and warm up. Don't delay.

When most of us hear a forecast that includes severe winter weather, we typically either plan on taking a day off from work or just figure that the commute will be a little slower than usual. Few of us anticipate things going seriously wrong and getting stuck in a car somewhere. But it can happen, and it only takes a small bit of time and effort to prep your car for a possible winter emergency. Here's what you should have on board when the weather gets frosty   .

CELL PHONE CHARGER Even in the best of weather, we've all ended up with a dead phone battery. Don't let it happen when you're stuck and potentially in danger.

WATER Safe drinking water is a critical item, even in winter. You don't have to be hot to dehydrate. Keep a gallon jug in your trunk for each person traveling in the car.

FLASHLIGHTS Keep several lights and some spare batteries. A headband light can be especially useful, keeping your hands free while you work on a broken-down car or rummage through the trunk in the dark.

FLARES These can be used to signal roadside distress and also to start a survival fire to stay warm if need be.

JUMPER CABLES Car batteries will be especially vulnerable in winter months.

TOW STRAP A nylon tow strap can help get your vehicle out of a ditch or snowbank.

FIRST AID KIT Sometimes the vehicle will need repair, and sometimes it's a person who needs mending.

FULL-SIZE SPARE, TIRE IRON, AND JACK Check your tires often in winter. If roads are snowy and icy, you can have a flat and not even know it.

SLEEPING BAGS If you've got a four-person car, carry four sleeping bags.

FOOD You probably don't need to stock up on heavy dinner items, but high-energy treats are great.

WINTER EXTRAS There are any number of extra items to help keep you comfortable if you're stranded in a car: a signal flag, tea candles, chemical hand warmers, and the like. When in doubt, include it.

36 DRIVE ON BLACK ICE

One of the most deadly results of freezing rain is the formation of black ice on the roadways. Of course it isn't actually black; this form of ice is so named because it creates a clear glaze on the pavement, making it very difficult to spot. Your best strategy for driving on black ice is not to, but sometimes you'll hit it unexpectedly. Be ready—never use cruise control on wet or icy roads.

STAY CALM When you feel your car losing traction, the worst thing you can do is panic and overreact, which could send your car into a potentially fatal spin.

DO LITTLE The best course is usually to keep the steering wheel straight, keep your foot off the brakes, stay calm and breathe deeply, and hope your car glides forward over the ice without incident, as black ice patches rarely extend for more than 20 feet (6 m).

CORRECT CAREFULLY If you feel your back end starting to slide, turn the steering wheel as gently as you can into the direction of the skid. Turning it the opposite direction can lead to a spinout.

EASE OFF You never want to brake, but you can slow down by taking your foot off of the accelerator. If you can, shift into low gear.

37 DRIVE IN A BLIZZARD

Driving in a snowstorm is like trying to steer with a pillowcase over your head. It's bad enough during daylight, but it gets really hairy at night when you turn on your headlights, because every snowflake reflects the light back into your eyes. And it's not only you: Everybody else out there is blind, too.

If a snowstorm escalates, pull to the side of the road. Reduce your beams to parking lights to aid your own vision, and use emergency flashers to let other drivers know where you are. Stay inside the vehicle so you don't get clobbered by another car. When the weather clears enough to allow safe driving again, brush snow off the top of the vehicle so it doesn't slide down and impede your visibility. Clear snow away from headlights and taillights, as well as all the windows and exterior mirrors. You might need to dig out the tires to gain traction, so carry a folding shovel. Experienced winter drivers carry tire chains and know how to use them (practice ahead of time). Other traction aids may include wooden planks and kitty litter or sand.

DON'T PILE ON IN A PILEUP

Having to drive during a snowstorm is unavoidable sometimes, but even a brief period of heavy snow or strong winds that reduces visibility is dangerous on a densely packed highway.

Every few weeks during the winter, we hear stories about dozens of cars involved in a pileup on a highway somewhere in the northern United States or Canada. All it takes is one person losing control of their vehicle to begin a chain reaction that can mangle dozens of cars and ruin hundreds of lives. Pileups are most common when visibility is near zero or roads are too icy for tires to maintain traction, leaving one car to slide into the one in front of it.

Avoid driving during a winter storm in the first place, but if you absolutely must, leave plenty of room between you and those around you. If you're involved in a pileup, you're in danger whether you stay in your vehicle or get out, unfortunately. However, getting out of your vehicle is the safest option—but only when there's no traffic behind you. Don't stay with your car—get as far off the road as possible so you're not a sitting duck when more cars creep up and crash alongside you. Head for safety, and leave a note on the car with your cell phone number so authorities can reach you. If there's no shelter, stay nearby.

39 DRINK SNOW

While you probably won't hurt yourself snacking on snow (unless it's contaminated or you've been following the sled dogs a little too closely), it's not a good idea for hydration. In a survival situation, trying to consume snow will make your body burn energy you don't have to spare. To make drinkable water, choose ice over snow if possible. Ice usually contains fewer foreign objects that can carry pathogens, and it will convert to more water than an equal volume of snow. Here are three ways to fill your water bottle from the cold stuff.

DRIP IT To melt snow or ice, snip a pea-size hole in the bottom corner of a T-shirt, pillowcase, or other makeshift fabric bag. Pack the bag with snow and hang it near a fire. Place a container under the hole to catch water melted by radiant heat. To keep the fabric from burning, refill the bag as the snow or ice melts.

COOK IT Melting your ice or snow in a pan risks scorching the pot, which will give the water a burned taste. Avoid this by heating a small amount of "starter water" from your water bottle before adding snow or ice. Place the pot over a low flame or just a few coals and agitate frequently.

HUG IT You may have no other option than to use body heat to melt the snow. If so, put small quantities of snow or ice in a waterproof container and then place the container between layers of clothing next to your body—but not against your skin. A soft plastic bag works better than a hard-shell canteen. Shake the container often to speed up the process.

40 MAKE SAFETY SPIKES

If you think there is any chance you might fall through a layer of ice and need to claw your way out, always be safe and carry a set of safety spikes with you. They're super easy to make, and can quite literally save your life should you find your self in trouble.

STEP 1 Wrap two Phillips-head screwdrivers in paracord and secure with strong knots, then coat them in foam tape for comfort and floatability.

STEP 2 Wear the spikes underneath your coat with the cord running up your arms and around your shoulders. Let the spikes dangle from your sleeves (or tuck them in your sleeves, if you prefer) when you're on the ice.

41 WATCH OUT WHEN THE SNOW MELTS

One of the scariest prospects after a season of heavy snow is the possible risk of temperatures rising just high enough to allow precipitation to fall as a cold rain instead of snow or even ice. A dense snowpack on the ground can be a recipe for disaster if a heavy rain threatens, as the rain will have few places to go unless all natural and man-made drainage systems are completely clear of snow and debris.

Once the heavy rain begins to fall onto a thick snowpack, it puddles anywhere it can, including against the walls of buildings and in parking lots. This scenario is particularly dangerous because it can cause roof collapses. Every winter, countless buildings, including homes and big-box stores, suffer roof damage from the weight of rain falling on top of accumulated snow.

The best way to prevent this kind of flooding and damage from winter rains is to clear any snow away from sewers and drainage pipes immediately after a storm. Try (safely, of course!) to remove any excess snow from your roof and gutters before it begins to melt or freeze, and before any rain falls, so you don't have to worry about your roof sustaining any leaks or structural damage from the weight of the slush.

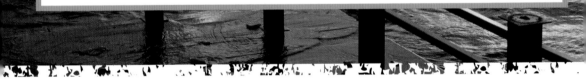

42 PRACTICE SIDEWALK SAFETY

An ice-covered walkway, path, or driveway is the perfect spot for bone-crunching wipeouts and unnecessary injuries. Does it make sense to salt your sidewalks and, if so, with what?

Table salt, Epsom salts, and rock salt will melt ice and you may already have them lying around the kitchen or garage. They are, however, harmful to the plants, shrubs, trees, and grass around the walkway, as well as potentially hazardous to pets and livestock who may try to eat them. Before the bad weather arrives, buy a bag of pet-friendly, lawn-friendly product that is made from magnesium chloride, calcium chloride, or related compounds. These are safer and less corrosive forms of salt than sodium chloride (table salt).

You don't actually have to melt the ice to make your sidewalk passable. Sand, gravel, sawdust, crushed nut shells, nonclumping cat litter, and wood ashes can give your feet traction on icy surfaces. They're better for the environment, and they are either cheap or free.

43 BE READY FOR STORMS

During horrific storms and tornadoes, all of your preparedness can be irrelevant. Bodily harm is often the biggest danger from these intense natural disasters. Have all the supplies as directed in this book, but keep in mind that they could all be blown into the next county. Head for a basement, root cellar, or, ideally, a buried storm shelter if you hear about an impending storm. If those locations aren't an option, hide in a closet in your home's interior, keeping the clothes in place as protection from storm-driven projectiles. You also could lie in a bathtub, covered in protective piles of towels, clothes, or bedding.

44 GET OUT OF THE MUD

During and after flooding, silt and mud make driving difficult, and you risk getting bogged down in mud. Likely, your vehicle will sink to the axles and refuse to move. Even if you're prepared, it will take time and effort to free your vehicle. Here's how to get moving again.

GET OFF THE GAS Spinning your tires will only end up digging deeper ruts and tossing around the remaining solid ground under the wheels.

GO BACK AND FORTH Switch between reverse and first gear to rock the vehicle; the wheels may pick up enough traction to get you out. Try it a few times.

DIG A PATH Using whatever tools you have on hand, hollow out a hole in the mud in front of each tire. Give each hole a slightly upward slope, then drive forward very gently and, with any luck, up the incline.

MAKE TRACTION Search your vehicle and the surrounding environment for items such as branches, gravel, blankets, or even your floor mats, and lay them immediately ahead of the wheels. Then gently drive over these objects onto firmer ground.

KEEP MOVING Once free, don't stop until you're back on firm ground.

45

STOP HYDROPLANING

When tires encounter more water than the tread grooves can dissipate, the tire essentially floats on a layer of water. That's hydroplaning—and it ain't a good thing for anybody.

READ THE CLUES When hydroplaning, the vehicle's engine will rev, so its revolutions per minute (RPM) will sharply increase. Simultaneously, the wheels will lose traction.

EASE UP Don't turn the wheel or hit the brakes; either will cause a skid. Instead, hold your course and ease off the accelerator, allowing your vehicle to slow down and the tires to penetrate the water layer.

46

DRIVE SAFELY IN HEAVY RAIN

While driving in the rain won't be as white-knuckle terrifying as being on the road while in a blizzard or hailstorm, it's not exactly safe or fun either, with the slippery streets and low visibility. Below are a few things to keep in mind. But remember, if the rain is coming down so hard you can't see, the safest thing to do is to pull as far off the road as possible and wait for it to pass. Turn on your hazard lights so you're not hit by someone trying to do the same thing!

SLOW DOWN Yes, it's obvious. It's also important. Even great drivers can still end up in crashes due to slippery roads, low visibility, and all those other drivers who aren't as awesome as you. It's a good rule of thumb to keep more than three seconds of distance between you and the car you're following in bad weather. So ride those brakes with pride.

DON'T PUDDLE JUMP Never drive straight through a large puddle unless you are absolutely 100 percent sure how deep it is (like, you just saw another car drive through it). It might be concealing a car-killer of a pothole or be deep enough that the water could damage your electrical system.

DOUBLE TAP That being said, when you do go driving through a big puddle, tap your brake pedal lightly to help dry your rotors.

DON'T GET SWEPT AWAY Never try to drive through running water. Every year, places with heavy rainfall have stories of cars getting stuck or even swept away when trying to cross seemingly insignificant water obstacles.

Sometimes you may not be able to wait around for someone to build a safe water crossing. Fording swift-moving water can be dangerous, but if you apply some basic triangular geometry, it can help you cross safely. If you are braving the current and you are backed up by two friends on shore—with a sturdy loop of rope twice the width of the body of water connecting all three of you—the two on land will be able to help you, even if you lose your footing. Once you reach the far bank, the second can cross, using the rope stretched between the banks as a safety line. When the last person is ready to cross, he or she can enter the water and be pulled across by the two on the far shore holding the rope.

Other tips for safety: face upstream while you cross, leave your shoes on to protect your feet and give you better grip, shuffle your feet along the bottom, and avoid lifting your feet. If the conditions are not favorable at one site, look for a better spot to cross.

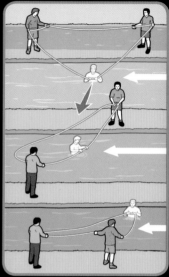

48 FIGHT BACK AGAINST FLOODING

Staying safe during a flood takes a combination of proper planning and quick thinking.

BE READY If you have enough warning, move important things to the highest and driest location in your home. Pack important and irreplaceable papers, photos, files, and data to take with you if you evacuate.

BE AWARE Monitor flood watches and warnings for your local area and areas upriver.

MOVE FAST Don't waste time packing. Things can be replaced, lives cannot. Move to higher ground if authorities say flash flooding is possible.

STOCK WATER Contamination can be a big deal during and after a flood, so make sure you have a safe supply of a gallon of water per person per day (don't forget pets!).

BUG OUT RIGHT Be prepared to evacuate. Keep your car stocked with cash, no-cook foods, spare clothes, sanitation items, your phone charger, rain gear, and other essentials in case you have to provide for your family for some time.

DO AS YOU'RE TOLD Never decide that you're smarter than the experts. If you are told to evacuate: DO IT!

DRIVE SAFELY Never drive through even the shallowest floodwaters—turn around and find another path. Even seemingly safe water can pick up your car and sweep it away.

49

RESCUE SOMEONE CAUGHT IN A FLOOD

The fast current of a flash flood is one of its biggest dangers. But if you're trying to help someone who's trapped by a flash flood—clinging to a tree branch or perched on the roof of a car—try using that speed to your advantage.

STEP 1 Tie a rescue rope to a solid object (a tree, for example) to anchor it against the weight of the victim and the flowing water's immense pressure.

STEP 2 Coil the rescue rope and throw it upstream of the person you're trying to rescue, allowing the current to carry the line down to the victim. Instruct the stranded person to tie the rope around his or her waist.

STEP 3 Once he or she is secured to the rope, the victim can leave the precarious perch and work toward the shore.

 FILL SANDBAGS CORRECTLY

Sandbags are often crucial in efforts to keep floodwaters at bay, diverting water from buildings and streets; and creating temporary dikes, levees, and other barriers.

Sandbags can be made of burlap or one of several sturdy artificial fabrics that will last about eight months to a year outside in the sun before needing to be replaced.

Sandbags can be stockpiled and transported by emergency workers, but it's much more common that they be filled as needed on site. This means that they're often being filled by volunteers and other civilians working alongside trained emergency workers. The bags can be filled with local sand, soil, or whatever's available.

Manually filling, moving, and stacking sandbags is physically demanding work. Because this vital task involves repeatedly lifting and carrying heavy bags, it's best done in small groups. The optimal work team is four people, though it can be done with fewer if necessary.

Each group should have a bagger, a shoveler, and a mover. The fourth person rotates into the group as necessary when

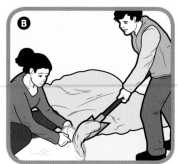

one person needs a break or a little extra assistance.

STEP 1 Make sure everyone is wearing work gloves, especially the person serving as bagger; his or her hands can be injured by the shovel during filling.

STEP 2 The bagger should crouch with his or her feet apart and arms extended, the bottom of the empty bag resting on the ground in front (A). Next, the bagger folds the open end of

the bag outward a few inches (7.5 cm) to form a collar.

STEP 3 While the bagger holds the mouth of the bag open, the shoveler carefully places sand into the bag (B), filling it no more than halfway (C).

STEP 4 If the bags are going to be transported, tie them shut tightly (D). Otherwise, move them to the stacking area as is, or add the bag directly to a wall in process.

51 PREP YOUR ATTIC

In flood-prone areas, the attic space inside your home can become the most important room in the house. Instead of storing your vital food, supplies, water, and gear at ground level (or worse, in a basement), you can create an ark out of that creepy, dusty attic. Following the ark theme a little further, you also should keep an inflatable raft in the attic to act as a floating storage shelf or means of exit. Have an ax up there, too—or, better yet, a chainsaw. Now you can cut your way out and make an aquatic escape. Remember to cut only a few trusses, to keep the roof from falling in. Wear safety glasses to keep sawdust and shingle grit out of your eyes.

52 DEAL WITH A FLOODED BASEMENT

A flooded basement is not only a hassle, it's potentially fatal. If there is any standing water, assume it's a dangerous electrical hazard. Before venturing in, have an electrician turn off the power at the meter (much safer than just turning off circuits, but it must be done by a professional). If there are gas appliances in the basement, shut off the gas main until the basement has been cleared.

Once it's safe to enter the basement, the easiest way to drain it is to rent a pump or have a service do it for you. There will likely be extensive property damage, and the risk of mold means that you'll need to properly dehumidify and rehabilitate the space. This can be complex, time-consuming, and expensive. If you don't have the experience to handle it right, hire professionals.

To prevent or limit damage, protect property by placing it on shelves in watertight containers. Keep nonwaterproof items at least 3 inches (7.5 cm) off the floor.

Install any electrical outlets and equipment high up and elevate the main breaker or fuse box and the utility meters above the anticipated flood level.

Install ground-fault interrupter (GFI) outlets as required by electrical code, and never leave extension cords on the floor.

53

RETURN HOME SAFELY AFTER A FLOOD

After the all-clear sounds, you'll want to rush back home and assess the damage. But even once the waters recede, you may still be in danger. Follow these basic guidelines to stay safe:

CHECK OUT STRUCTURAL INTEGRITY If your foundation or roof looks damaged, wait for an inspector to check out your home's stability before you go back inside.

CHECK FOR GAS LEAKS After all you've been through, you probably don't want to deal with an explosion as well. If the lights are out, don't light a candle. Turn off the gas main and then remain outside. Have the fire department or gas utility check your home before entering to be sure it is safe.

HANDLE ELECTRICITY Turn off the power at the main circuit breaker or fuse box with something nonconductive, such as a broom or a rolled-up rubber mat. Wearing rubber gloves is also smart.

KEEP APPLIANCES OFF Have an electrician check out anything electrical or motorized that got wet.

DRAIN THE BASEMENT SLOWLY Emptying a flooded basement all at once can damage your home's stability. Drain a third of the water volume per day.

54

ASSESS YOUR HOME AFTER A FLOOD

Once you're sure your home is safe to enter (see item 53, above), you'll want to take inventory of the damage. Follow these guidelines:

BE SURE OF STABILITY Doors stuck in frames could be a sign your foundation or roof is damaged.

AIR IT OUT If there is a strong smell of gas or if you hear a hissing sound, immediately exit, opening any doors or windows as you leave to air out the house. Even if you do not smell gas, open doors and windows to air out your home. Assist in drying the interior by using fans and dehumidifiers to help remove excess moisture.

SPOT SAGGING Check the ceiling and floor for any signs of sagging. Water may be trapped in the ceiling, or floors may be unsafe to walk on.

55 TACKLE WATER DAMAGE

If your home has suffered water damage from flooding, it will be prone to a mold infestation, which can develop after only 24–48 hours.

DRY OUT Set up fans and dehumidifiers, and move wet items away from walls and off the floors. Find the source of the moisture and stop it from worsening the problem.

TOSS THE TRASH Items that have absorbed moisture and have mold growing on them need to be thrown out. Remove the sheetrock a level above the high-water mark of any flooding. Any porous material that shows visible signs of mold should be thrown away.

CLEAN UP Surface mold growing on nonporous materials can usually be cleaned. Thoroughly scrub contaminated surfaces with hot water, a nonammonia soap, detergent, or commercial cleaner. Use a stiff brush to scrub all contaminants. Rinse with clean water and collect the excess rinse water and detergent with a wet/dry vacuum, a mop, or a sponge.

DISINFECT Apply a bleach solution or antimicrobial cleaner to surfaces that show mold growth. An effective way to eliminate mold and musty smells in large or inaccessible spaces is to use a "cold fogger," which distributes a mold-control mist throughout the space, even in hard-to-access areas.

LOOK OUT Be alert to the signs that mold may be returning to areas of past infestation. If it does return, repeat cleaning steps or, in cases of heavy infestation, seek professional help.

HIGH WIND ADVISORY

TRY NOT TO GET BLOWN AWAY.

A light spring breeze on the cheek is a beautiful thing, but when the wind power picks up and turns into a freight train—or begins to whorl into a vortex—it can turn deadly. Depending on where in the world you live, you may be subject to tornadoes, hurricanes, or typhoons. The end result of these super-powered winds can range from downed trees to crushed homes and buildings to massive flooding. High winds can come on suddenly, but with preparation, you can stand firm. It may mean battening down the hatches, and it may mean knowing how to evacuate safely. This chapter shows you how to weather any kind of windstorm—of any speed—that comes blasting your way.

56 PREPARE FOR HURRICANES AND CYCLONES

Getting ready for a hurricane can be a little intimidating, but it accomplishes two vital things. First, preparing for trouble removes some of the helplessness that many people feel when an emergency is imminent, putting you in the right mind-set: to be a survivor, not a victim. Second, prepping forces you to gather the supplies and make the plans that can help you adapt to the changing environment of a disaster. This can even arm you with the security and resources to help others as you put the pieces back together after a storm.

As you prepare for a hurricane, consider that you may lose power, which obviously takes away many of our modern conveniences. Make sure you have plenty of easy-to-fix, no-cook foods on hand and ample sources of lighting. Lean toward battery-operated lights instead of candles to reduce the hazard of fire. Also, make sure you know the routes to evacuate inland, away from the hurricane's path.

Gather at least a 72-hour supply of water and food for each person in your home, plus flashlights, first-aid supplies, hygiene items, and something to pass the time for each person (books, board games, coloring books for the kids, and other electricity-free items). Get your cell phone charged up, and have a backup power source for it, like a car charger or external battery packs. Also have a battery-powered radio so you can stay alert to evacuation notices, disaster news, and other instructions.

EVACUATION ROUTE

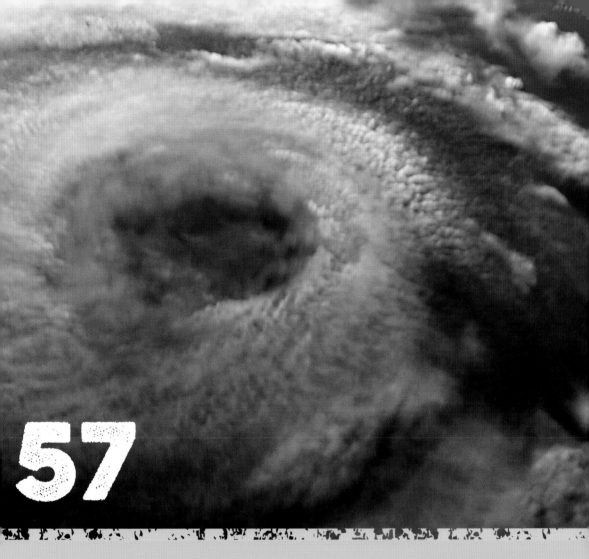

57

BEWARE THE EYE OF THE STORM

The middle of each hurricane has a calm "eye" that can give the false impression that the storm is over. Often the worst part of the storm happens after the eye passes and the winds begin to blow from the opposite direction. Trees, buildings, and other objects damaged by the first part of the storm can be further damaged or destroyed by the second winds. Opposing winds begin suddenly, injuring unsuspecting people who left their shelter before they received an "all clear" from local emergency management officials.

58

CATEGORIZE THAT HURRICANE

We love to use scales to figure out how one major disaster compares to others in objective terms. It's one thing to say that a hurricane had 145 mph (233 km/h) winds, but when you instead say, "the hurricane was a Category 4," locals instantly get an idea of what kind of damage the winds could produce. The Saffir-Simpson Hurricane Wind Scale was introduced in the mid 1970s by Herbert Saffir, an American civil engineer, and Robert Simpson, a meteorologist, in order to estimate the amount of damage a hurricane could be expected to produce on landfall. Just based on winds, a category 1 hurricane would cause much less damage than a Category 5.

While the Saffir-Simpson scale is a useful tool for quickly and effectively communicating hurricane risk to the public, it does have its disadvantages. Winds are only part of the equation—residents who are facing and trying to evaluate the threat of a hurricane have to take into account the risk for flooding and/or a storm surge (defined as an abnormal rise of water generated by a storm, over and above the predicted astronomical tide), as well as the possibility of tornadoes in addition to the winds. Hurricane Sandy was "only" a Category 1 when it made landfall in the northeastern United States, but its immense storm surge devastated hundreds of miles of coastline from New Jersey to Rhode Island.

	SPEED	DAMAGE	TYPE OF DAMAGE	EXAMPLE
CATEGORY 1	74-95 mph (119-153 km/h)	Widespread	Branches and limbs down, damage to gutters, shingles, and siding.	Hurricane Irene (2011)
CATEGORY 2	96-110 mph (154-177 km/h)	Severe	Widespread roof damage occurs; extensive power outages.	Hurricane Arthur (2014)
CATEGORY 3	111-129 mph (178-208 km/h)	Extreme	Most buildings damaged, some homes destroyed.	Hurricane Katrina (2005)
CATEGORY 4	130-156 mph (209-251 km/h)	Catastrophic	Most buildings damaged, some homes destroyed.	Hurricane Charley (2004)
CATEGORY 5	157+ mph (252+ km/h)	Complete devastation	Equivalent to a violent tornado. Devastation likely. Area uninhabitable for an extended period of time.	Hurricane Andrew (1992)

59

DRIVE IN HIGH WINDS

When you discount the threats of flying debris and falling trees, strong winds are less of a hazard inside vehicles than they are outside, but crosswinds can still make it very hard (if not impossible) to control your vehicle. You'll also have to contend with the fact that visibility will be very low—if not zero—along with the possibility that high-profile vehicles like box trucks or 18-wheelers will tip over under the enormous force of strong winds (and there are lots of those on the road). Here are some basic tips if you can't get off the road and the winds are rising fast.

SLOW DOWN It's tempting to want to get off the highway as quickly as possible—and maybe even a little exhilarating if the wind's behind you. But your ability to correct when that same wind shifts its direction and pushes you off course is somewhat limited. High wind reduces friction. It causes your car to lift a bit, it shoves the car off its line, and it's often accompanied by rain. None of this is good for your control of the vehicle.

STAY AWAY FROM TRAILERS Whether we're talking about those 18-wheelers, or boats on trailers, or a basic U-Haul™, the fact is the driver has very little control over what happens to that trailer in a high wind, and the whole thing probably has a high nonaerodynamic profile. Stay back.

WATCH FOR DEBRIS Tree limbs may be blown onto the road, soil embankments may slide into your lane, and that idiot who hasn't tied his mattress down is really regretting that decision. Another reason to take it slow.

60 COPE WITH A POWER LINE

You really shouldn't be out driving in a major storm. You do know that, right? But sometimes it happens. And sometimes the truly unexpected and terrifying happens. That's the case for those unlucky few folks who have happened to be driving by right as the wind took out a nearby power pole. If a power line falls on your car and disables it while you're inside, you'll have to take action. But what on earth to do?

PUT OUT AN S.O.S. The safest thing to do is to remain in your vehicle and phone for help.

JUMP FREE If you absolutely must leave the vehicle because of fire or some other danger, avoid touching any portion of your car's metal frame. The greatest peril will come from touching the car and the ground at the same time, because electricity could travel through you into the ground, causing injury or death. Jump as far away from the car as you can, landing with your feet together.

SHUFFLE OFF TO SAFETY Keep feet in contact with each other and the ground as you move away. Avoid water, which conducts electricity.

61 BRACE FOR DEADLY WINDS

When you can look up at the sky from your living room and wonder where your roof went, it feels like splitting hairs to try to figure out the pattern of the winds that blew the cap off your house. Damaging winds are damaging winds, after all, but they can come from very different beasts, and you should probably know what you'll be facing in your area.

	HOW THEY MOVE	DAMAGE	SIGNS
STRAIGHT-LINE WINDS	As you might guess, in a straight line. The strongest straight-line winds can exceed hurricane force.	Usually cause damage to trees, power lines, loose objects, and vulnerable structures like old barns or poorly constructed backyard forts and sheds.	Blow everything in the same direction like a giant, airy steamroller.
TORNADIC WINDS	Spin around in a circular fashion.	Can cause more damage than straight-line winds; debris gets more opportunities to destroy other objects, creating more flying debris, and so on.	Deposit debris in a circular pattern—sometimes even creating cycloidal markings, or swirling scars, in the earth itself.

62 DON'T GET BLOWN AWAY

Some of the strongest hurricanes produce winds equivalent to what you'd see in a powerful tornado, just over a much, much larger area. A Category 5 hurricane can pack the same intensity as a high-end EF-3 tornado (see item 73), but over dozens of miles instead of a few thousand feet.

STRUCTURAL DAMAGE The most serious wind damage occurs to buildings. Damage is highly dependent on how well the building is constructed—modern school buildings, for instance, can withstand much higher winds than single-family homes. Weaker hurricanes cause mostly superficial damage, such as tearing off siding and shingles, but otherwise don't compromise the integrity of the building. Damage to gabled roofs and garages can facilitate destruction of the building—if garage doors fail, wind can get in and tear it apart from the inside out, compromising the rest of the house. Similar damage can occur when a roof fails, weakening the structure and allowing damaging winds to more easily tear away at walls and support beams.

FALLING TREES Damage caused by winds increases steadily with greater speed. A pocket of 80 mph (129 km/h) sustained winds will result in less damage than 140 mph (225 km/h) winds, of course, but each is dangerous if your home is in the path of a tree that comes crashing to the ground. Trees can withstand a surprising amount of force, but their ability to stand up to a hurricane depends on factors such as height, foliage, root systems, soil moisture, and tree health. If you live in a building surrounded by tall trees, it would be a good idea to evacuate to safer shelter if you can.

WIND-BORNE PERIL Flying debris is a significant threat to those caught outside during strong winds. Never venture outside during a hurricane, even if you think it's safe to do so. It just takes one small flying object nailing you just right to make you wish you had stayed inside.

63

NEVER TRY TO OUTRUN THE SURGE

While water is surging ashore, your options are very limited. Basically, get to the highest point you can and hope it's higher than the peak of the surge. In Hurricane Katrina, some people drowned in their homes because the surge filled the rooms so quickly that they couldn't escape. Water can rise 6 to 10 feet (2-3 m) in minutes—faster if it's filling an enclosed space.

Still, people try to outrun the surge in their cars. The logic behind this mistake is thinking since you can drive through an inch (1.5 cm) of water, as long as you drive fast enough, you can get away before it rises higher.

The fact is that if you wait until the water is an inch (2.5 cm) high before trying to outrun the surge, it will likely rise to over a foot high before you can even get your car out of the driveway. If the water is a foot high and traveling at 10 to 15 mph (16-24 km/h), it can easily sweep a car away. Don't risk it.

64 DON'T GO UNDER

Wind speeds sound dramatic, but the storm surge is the more lethal threat. A storm surge occurs when a hurricane's winds push ocean water onto land, creating a flood that can be tens of feet deep and reach several miles inland. If you've ever watched strong winds blow across the surface of a pool or a pond, you can see the small waves focus their energy on one end of the body of water. If the winds are strong enough, you can even see the small waves push over the edge of the pool or pond.

BIG BLOW Tropical cyclones can have wind fields that extend more than 100 miles (160 km) from the storm's center—this mass of violent winds takes a great toll on the surface of the ocean, pushing along a bubblelike surge of water ahead of it. When the cyclone makes

landfall, this bubble of water piles up on the coast and starts to push inland. Most storm surges rise from nothing to a catastrophe in a matter of hours, and the vast majority of people who die from hurricanes in the United States die as a direct result of storm surges.

TINY TERROR Even marginal tropical storms can produce a small storm surge, the effects of which vary widely depending on a number of factors. Most surges are only a few feet deep, affecting communities immediately on the coast, but a storm hitting the wrong area can wreak havoc. Hurricane Sandy only had winds of about 80 mph (129 km/h) at landfall, but its wind field was so large that it pushed a devastating surge into the U.S. East Coast, especially in and around New York City.

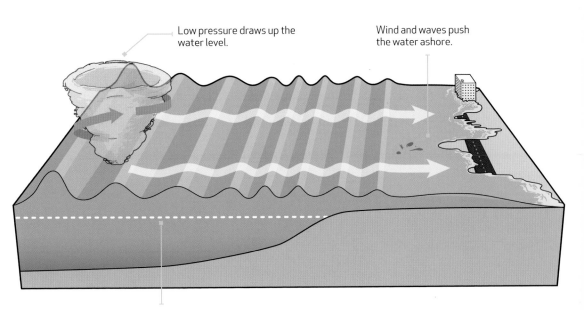

Low pressure draws up the water level.

Wind and waves push the water ashore.

Normal sea level

65 MAKE YOUR GARAGE WIND RESISTANT

Battening down the hatches to prepare for a storm? Don't forget the garage. Double-wide garage doors are a weak spot in a windstorm, as high winds can cause these broad, flexible doors to bow inward and even fall off their tracks. And that makes your garage, car, and home vulnerable to greater damage from flying debris and falling objects.

You could invest in a wind-resistant door, or reinforce the current door yourself with a kit that will allow you to brace your door and still use it. But if a high-wind advisory has just been issued and you have to act fast, you can board up your garage door with wooden planks, just as you would your home's windows. Add horizontal and vertical bracing onto each panel of the door. If you have an automatic garage-door opener, disable it to avoid accidental damage from someone trying to open the door while it's boarded up.

2x4s make ideal braces.

Create a "hook" by nailing a short section of 2x4s to the wall. Then attach the hook to the bracing with a screw.

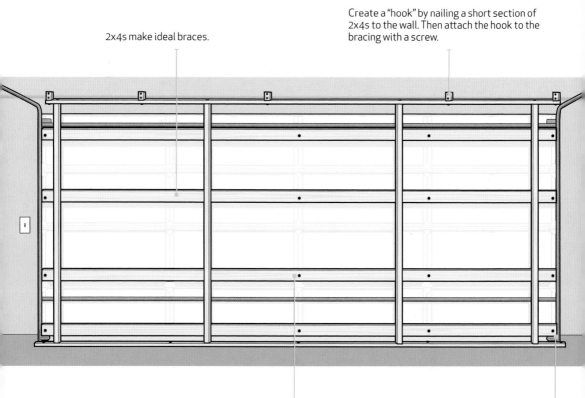

For extra security, nail the braces into the door's studs.

The horizontal boards should be flush with the door's track.

66 MINIMIZE WIND DAMAGE TO YOUR HOME

How can wind damage a home? The most common form of damage is largely superficial, when gusty winds blow away roofing materials like shingles or tiles, tear off vinyl siding, or cause screens, gutters, and any other decorative items to come loose and fly away in the torrent of air. More serious damage can occur when winds exceed hurricane force, and airborne debris shatters windows, damages walls, or even weakens and eventually tears away the entire roof. Poorly constructed buildings and those made from lightweight materials (like mobile or prefab homes) can be completely destroyed by very strong straight-line winds. This diagram shows you how you can protect your home. If you're unsure how to check these things, it's worth it to have a home inspector give your house a once-over. Your insurance company may offer this service or be able to recommend a good resource.

Do not drain or cover your pool.

Cover all windows, sliding-glass doors, French doors, and skylights with storm shutters to prevent broken glass.

Ensure shingles are firmly nailed down and well fitted.

Check roof sheathing is securely nailed down.

Be sure the connection between roof and walls is tight enough to keep updrafts from lifting off the roof.

Garage doors should be properly braced.

Be sure lawn furniture, toys, garbage bins, and other items that might become projectiles in a high wind are securely stowed or battened down before a storm.

Any tree that might threaten your home should be safely pruned or, worst case, removed entirely.

All external doors should have a deadbolt.

Be sure all cracks are well sealed. This keeps you warm and saves energy, but it also ensures wind doesn't cause interior damage.

67 TREE-PROOF YOUR HOME

Large, mature trees can help increase the value of your property—unless they crash into your house after a major storm. If you live somewhere frequently hit by windy storms, it's likely to happen eventually. Prune weak, damaged, or dead limbs, and ask your local power company if they have a program for pruning.

CULL THE HERD The best way to tree-proof your home is to remove all trees from your yard that could reach your house if they were to fall.

PLANT DEFENSIVELY Saplings planted today will eventually grow up to become trees that might pose a danger to your house. Pick spots where the trees won't threaten your home, your neighbor's house, or external features like power lines and propane tanks. Don't plant brittle species that break easily, such as elm, willow, box elder, poplar, and silver maple. Where ice storms are a possibility, don't plant trees that hold their leaves late into the fall. The weight of ice on leaves can bring down limbs or entire trees.

ASK NICELY If the tree that's looming over your house should belong to your neighbors, use diplomacy to get them to remove it. That task will be easier if you can convince them that the tree is a danger to their house, too.

68 DEAL WITH A DOWNED TREE

When severe weather hits, downed trees follow. Make like a lumberjack and use the proper technique to cut up a tree on the ground—a process called bucking.

STEP 1 Remove all major branches, then brace the underside of the tree with wood to keep it stable and off the ground.

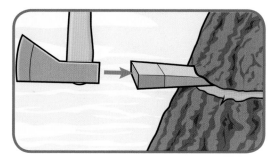

STEP 3 Gravity should pull that trunk section off the tree, but if your saw gets stuck in the cut, shut it off right away. Drive a wedge into the cut to loosen the tension, and then remove the saw.

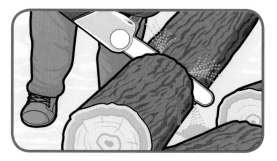

STEP 2 Standing uphill from the tree, start by cutting the underside of the trunk about one-third of the way through with a chainsaw. Then come back to the top side and finish the cut so it runs all the way through the trunk.

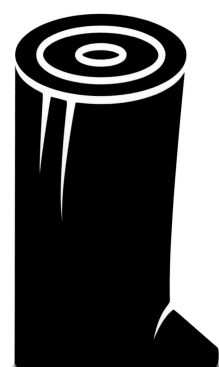

WATCH THE BIRTH OF A MONSTER

How does a tornado form? It's one of the many questions meteorologists are still trying to answer. We're creeping closer to the answer to this one, but we're not quite there yet. Scientists began studying tornadoes in earnest back in the middle of the 20th century, but with increasingly advanced equipment, we're getting a better handle on how thunderstorms generate these volatile creatures.

MEET THE PARENTS The two most common types of tornadoes we deal with are those generated by supercells and those spawned by squall lines. Tornadoes birthed by supercells are the classic twisters that we see chasers flocking toward on the plains. The most popular theory explains that the rear-flank downdraft—the rain-cooled air that sinks around the backside of a supercell—can pull

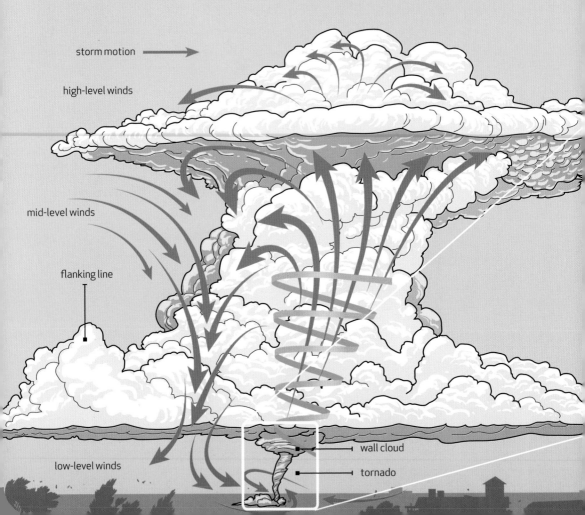

storm motion

high-level winds

mid-level winds

flanking line

low-level winds

wall cloud

tornado

the thunderstorm's mesocyclone toward the ground, causing it to stretch and spin faster (think of an ice skater pulling her arms in) as it approaches the surface.

LITTLE TERRORS Tornadoes that form along the leading edge of squall lines also account for a good percentage of twisters. Many meteorologists will refer to these as weak, "spin-up" tornadoes, as they tend to be small, short-lived, and contain winds that only produce minor amounts of damage. Don't be lulled into a false sense of security by these terms. Even a small tornado can be dangerous if you're caught out unprepared

and unprotected. So be prepared, even if what's coming is tiny compared to the true monster storms.

LOOK INSIDE The inner workings of a tornado are complicated, with violent winds almost always swirling counterclockwise in the Northern Hemisphere and clockwise in the Southern. Tornadoes also have an upward component to them, with winds in the center racing skyward through the tornado and into the core of the storm. They can suck debris high into the upper atmosphere; small objects like envelopes and photographs can travel hundreds of miles downwind.

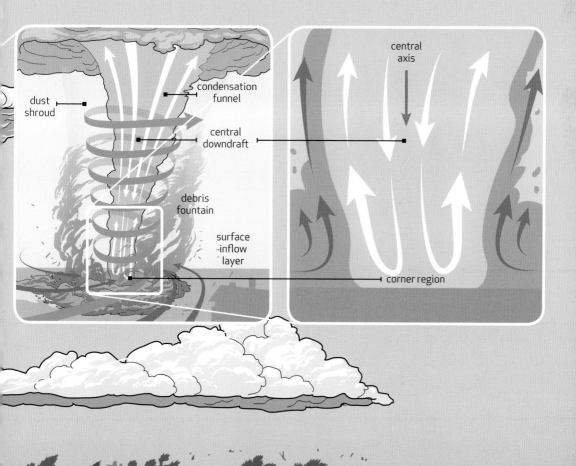

dust shroud

condensation funnel

central downdraft

debris fountain

surface -inflow layer

central axis

corner region

70 SPOT TORNADO WARNING SIGNS

Is that shape on the horizon an innocent cloud—or a deadly tornado? As you scan the skies, keep an eye out for these signs.

SUPERCELL Look out for a looming thunderhead with a hard-edged, cauliflower look. This is a supercell: a dangerous formation that can produce interior winds of up to 170 mph (274 km/h).

WALL CLOUD These look dense and sort of like a wall with clearly defined edges.

GREEN TINGE While there's some debate about whether this is folklore, many say that a sickly green hue in the sky can mean a tornado is taking shape.

FUNNEL CLOUD A needlelike formation that's descending from a cloud's base indicates its rotation. When a funnel cloud touches the ground, it becomes a tornado—luckily most never touch down.

STRANGE SOUNDS Listen up for any sounds like swarming bees or a waterfall—these may be an approaching twister you're hearing. If your ears pop, there's been a drop in air pressure, which is another danger sign.

Supercell

Green Tinge

Wall Cloud

Funnel Cloud

71

AVOID TORNADO ALLEY

The United States is ground zero for the most violent tornadoes in the world; in fact, more than three-quarters of all the tornadoes that touch down every year occur in the United States. Warm, moist air pumping in from the Gulf of Mexico and cold winds aloft blowing in from the west often create the perfect mixture of moisture, instability, and wind shear for big twisters.

SOUTHERN EXPOSURE

Tornado Alley is a swath of the central U.S. that serves as a breeding ground for tornado outbreaks. Its flat terrain and favorable storm tracks allow Tornado Alley to see violent twisters on a fairly regular basis. Another hot spot for tornadoes is "Dixie Alley," a region stretching from central Mississippi through northern Alabama and southeastern Tennessee. The worst tornado outbreak in U.S. history unfolded there. April 27, 2011, was the worst day of the outbreak, when more than 200 tornadoes killed more than 300 people and injured thousands.

ACROSS THE COUNTRY

Twisters have occurred in all 50 states. Some regions see few tornadoes, such as the deep Appalachian and Rocky Mountains, as well as portions of the West Coast, but they aren't immune. The state with the fewest tornadoes is Alaska; due to its cool and stable weather, and few residents around to see the twisters that do happen, only four tornadoes have been reported since 1950.

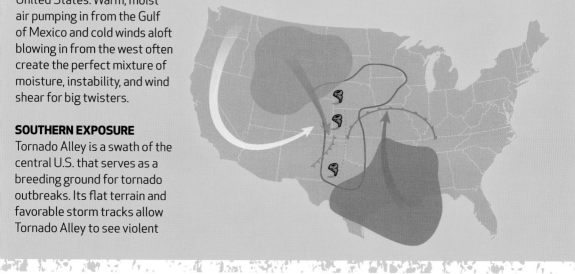

72

JUDGE WHERE A TORNADO IS HEADING

If you're on the ground, staring at a tornado, you can usually tell whether it's moving to your left or right. But if a tornado looks like it's standing still, you're right in its path—and you need to get out, quick!

Tornadoes often move from southwest to northeast, so you can use a compass or a car's navigation system to avoid driving in the same direction. Of course, nothing beats the eyeball test. If you see a tornado, drive at a right angle to its path. Don't try driving directly away from the twister—that'll put you exactly in the line of danger. There's an excellent chance that the tornado will overtake you, because twisters are difficult—sometimes impossible—to outrun.

73 RATE THE FURY

Attempting to directly measure the winds in a tornado is a dangerous and sometimes impossible task. The best way to estimate a tornado's strength is to study the damage it leaves behind. Dr. Theodore Fujita

EF-0

SEVERITY: Minor

RELATIVE FREQUENCY:
Most common

ESTIMATED WIND GUSTS:
65–85 mph (105-137 km/h)

DAMAGE EXPECTED:
Shingles blown off and minor roof damage possible; gutters and vinyl siding damaged. Tree branches and limbs felled, weak trees knocked over.

EF-1

SEVERITY: Moderate

RELATIVE FREQUENCY:
Common

ESTIMATED WIND GUSTS:
86–110 mph (138-177 km/h)

DAMAGE EXPECTED:
Windows broken, mobile or prefabricated homes severely damaged. Significant roof damage to well-built homes.

EF-2

SEVERITY: Considerable

RELATIVE FREQUENCY:
Common

ESTIMATED WIND GUSTS:
111–135 mph (178-217 km/h)

DAMAGE EXPECTED:
Roofs torn off; structural damage to homes possible. Mobile or prefabricated homes destroyed. Cars overturned.

was a world-renowned meteorologist who pioneered tornado research, and he developed the Fujita Scale (now the Enhanced Fujita or EF), which uses the damage caused to different types of buildings as a way to estimate a tornado's wind speed at a particular location. By studying the damage caused to a well-built wood-frame house, for instance, you can get a pretty accurate measure of how strong a tornado was.

EF-3

SEVERITY: Severe
RELATIVE FREQUENCY: Infrequent
ESTIMATED WIND GUSTS: 136–165 mph (218-266 km/h)
DAMAGE EXPECTED: Possible significant, irreparable damage to well-built structures. Top floors sheared off homes and businesses. Cars tossed through the air.

EF-4

SEVERITY: Extreme
RELATIVE FREQUENCY: Rare
ESTIMATED WIND GUSTS: 166–200 mph (267-322 km/h)
DAMAGE EXPECTED: Commercial buildings and homes leveled. Reinforced structures such as schools and prisons sustain serious damage.

EF-5

SEVERITY: Catastrophic
RELATIVE FREQUENCY: Exceptionally rare
ESTIMATED WIND GUSTS: 201+ mph (323+ km/h)
DAMAGE EXPECTED: Most buildings scrubbed to their foundation. Steel storage tanks may be sheared from their bolts. Vehicles mangled beyond recognition. Trees debarked. Grass and roads scoured from the earth.

74

KNOW WHEN TO WORRY

Almost more important than knowing where to seek shelter and what to do when a tornado is barreling toward you is to know in advance when one could potentially bear down on your location. Thanks to Doppler weather radar and dramatic advances in forecasting,

meteorologists can typically warn residents of a potential tornado 15 or more minutes before it strikes. The lead time is critical, as it allows you to put your safety plan into action.

TORNADO WATCH This type of alert means that conditions are favorable for the development of severe thunderstorms that are capable of producing tornadoes. Tornado watches are typically issued hours in advance of the arrival of thunderstorms, and they are meant to put residents on alert to pay hawk-like attention to the latest developments and updates.

TORNADO WARNING This stronger alert indicates that a tornado has been spotted or Doppler weather radar detects strong rotation that could lead to the imminent development of a tornado. Unlike a tornado watch, a tornado warning means the twister has touched down; you are in immediate danger and need to take swift action to save your life and the lives of those around you. Tornado warnings typically have a lead time of about 15 minutes, but this can be much shorter (or much longer) depending on the situation.

Meteorologists are experimenting with different terminology for tornado warnings to convey the relative severity of a situation. If spotters report that a violent tornado is moving into a populated area, meteorologists will upgrade a tornado warning to a tornado emergency, in an attempt to give people extra motivation to take lifesaving measures. This exceedingly rare designation was developed by the National Weather Service in Norman, Oklahoma, on May 3-4, 1999, when a violent EF-5 tornado tore through the southern suburbs of Oklahoma City, killing 40 people.

75

CALCULATE THE ODDS

Whether you are an adult, a child, or somewhere in the middle, being terrified of tornadoes is not unreasonable. It's natural and even healthy to fear these beastly whirlwinds, but for as much play as they get in the news, they're not as common as you might think.

Let's take a look at the numbers—they're actually more comforting than concerning. From the Florida Keys to the Puget Sound,

the United States can see more than 100,000 individual thunderstorms every year. The National Weather Service estimates that only 5 percent of all the thunderstorms that form in the country produce severe weather, and only about 1 percent of all thunderstorms go on to produce a tornado. Even if a thousand tornado-producing thunderstorms sounds like a lot, consider the fact that most tornadoes are only a few hundred feet wide and last for about 10 minutes at the most. That's a relatively small patch of real estate that's affected by these (admittedly powerful) vortices.

If it's strength you're worried about, consider the fact that only 0.1 percent of all tornadoes that have formed within the United States produced EF-5 damage—the highest rating used to estimate the intensity of a tornado. The majority of tornadoes (close to 90 percent) are between EF-0 and EF-2 intensity—strong enough to pose a serious threat to people who aren't protected but hardly enough to scour homes down to their foundations.

In short, it's always wise to prepare for the worst-case scenario, but odds are low that you'll ever directly experience a tornado in your lifetime.

76 SURVIVE ON THE ROAD

Sheltering in vehicles is a very risky gambit in a tornado, as cars can be tumbled or thrown by a strong twister. It really boils down to a choice of similar perils. If you see a tornado while you're driving in a car, and it's far away and you have open road ahead, then you might be able to outrun it by driving at a right angle to the tornado's path (if you can tell what that is). Of course, the smarter choice is to seek shelter indoors or underground if at all possible.

If you're caught in a vehicle and cannot drive, the best option is usually to abandon the vehicle. You're probably safer lying in a ditch than you are sitting in the car. If you do decide to stay in the car, or you don't have time to run to a ditch, keep your seat belt fastened, cover your head

with your hands, and use a jacket, coat, or some other covering to protect you from flying debris. The vehicle will be safer on a lower road level than a higher one or on a bridge.

That said, do not head for an overpass, no matter whether you've seen any movie characters or people in documentaries who do and live to tell about it. Aside from flying through the air, this is the worst place to be in a tornado. Let me be clear: It is not safe to take shelter under an overpass during a tornado. Overpasses do not provide protection—in fact, the air squeezing into the tight spaces under an overpass actually increases the tornado's wind speed, increasing the chance that you'll get sucked out or pelted with debris.

77 RIDE IT OUT IN THE OPEN

There is no good way to survive in the open, which is why paying attention to weather forecasts is so crucial. That said, if you do get caught outdoors and there is no sturdy shelter within running distance, these instructions (and a lot of luck) may help. Lie facedown in a low area. Protect the back of your head with your arms and any extra clothing you have. Don't try to hold onto a tree, or shelter near other seemingly solid objects. They may be blown onto you, or you may be scooped up and hurled at them.

78 SHELTER IN PLACE, PROPERLY

When a tornado threatens, the simplest advice is to get yourself to the safest and sturdiest spot that's close and easy to reach. No matter where you end up sheltering, use this basic body-protecting technique: Crouch down low with your face downward. Cover your head with your hands, or throw on a sports helmet for protection against head injury if at all possible. Wrap up in blankets or sleeping bags to pad against bodily injury, or flop a mattress on top of you for storm debris protection.

BASEMENT REFUGE If you're in a house with a basement, go down there and crawl under something sturdy. This could be a heavy table, a work bench, a mattress, or the like. Stay keenly aware of the position of heavy objects (like refrigerators, waterbeds, pianos, etc.) on the floor above the basement, and don't hang out under those spots. Also, avoid windows and sliding glass doors, as well as chimneys (which might collapse).

SMALL-SPACE SAFETY If you're in a space that has no basement, the first rule is to stay away from the windows. Go to a bathroom, closet, or a space under the stairs on the lowest floor. Failing that, get to an interior hallway with no windows. Jumping into a bathtub may offer partial protection, but cover up with some sort of thick padding, like a mattress or several blankets.

OUT IN PUBLIC If you're in a church, theater, mall, or large store, get to shelter as quickly as you can, such as an interior bathroom, a storage room, or other small enclosure away from any windows. If you're at school, follow the staff's instructions.

79 DON'T GO MOBILE

Every time a tornado whirls through the area, you flip on the news and hear a terrible, tragic story about how a family was killed when their mobile home was swept away in the fierce winds.

UNDERSTAND THE DANGER The two main weaknesses of these abodes are the open space under the trailer and the lightweight building materials. The space underneath can allow wind to blow under the trailer, which can end up flipping it or lifting it into the air. The lightweight construction that makes these dwellings mobile also enables the tornado to move them, occasionally shredding them into tiny pieces. Even small tornadoes can destroy tied-down mobile homes, and even the best-built and most modern of mobile homes and trailers aren't able to handle the high winds and incredible wrenching forces.

BE VIGILANT Mobile home dwellers need to take an extra level of precaution when heavy weather threatens. Be ready to go before the tornado warning sounds—preferably even before the watch does. That means watching the news on TV or online, and being ready to get up and go before the last minute. Better to run for town unnecessarily than to get caught in a whirling deathtrap.

GET TO SAFETY If you're caught in a mobile home during a tornado warning, your best bet is to quickly evacuate to a sturdier building for shelter, provided you can get there safely.

80 SEE A WORLD OF TROUBLE

Thanks to weather trends mixed with a dollop of cultural egotism, it seems like we only ever hear about tornadoes that form in the United States. There are some other hot spots for activity beyond our fruited plains. Bangladesh is particularly vulnerable, but you'll find twisters around the globe.

Tornado activity is possible almost anywhere in Europe during the stormy spring and summer months—northern Italy and portions of Germany and Poland often see several violent tornadoes a year.

South Africa and eastern Australia can also see a handful of raucous supercells every year, spawning picturesque tornadoes that tear through a mostly unpopulated landscape. Even Japan also is known to see a couple of tornadoes every year, which is especially dangerous given the high population densities in many of its cities.

Tornado Hot Spots

81 AVOID NASTY SURPRISES

One of the most overlooked threats during a hurricane is a tornado, which really adds insult to injury when you think about it. Small tornadoes are common in the fast-moving bands of showers and thunderstorms as they push ashore, resulting from the incredible amounts of low-level wind shear and rotation that can accompany tropical systems. Tornado outbreaks are common in storms that make landfall on the United States' Gulf Coast—several days after making landfall in Florida, 2004 Hurricane Ivan produced more than 100 tornadoes as it moved up the East Coast, killing several people and causing tens of millions of dollars in damage.

82 BEWARE THE HAILSTORM

Thunderstorms that drop frozen rain, aka hail, are often called hailstorms. Pellets of hail form when strong currents of air (called updrafts) carry water droplets to a height where they freeze. When the hail "stones" gather more moisture and grow too big to be supported by the updraft, they fall to the ground at speeds up to 100 mph (161 km/h). Hail tends to do more damage to property than to people, though deadly freak hailstorms have occurred throughout history. On a day that became known as "Black Monday" in 1360, a hailstorm killed approximately 1,000 English soldiers near Paris during the Hundred Years' War. And in the 9th century, near the town of Roopkund, India, several hundred pilgrims were killed by a massive hailstorm. Dealing with hail is easy: Seek shelter during thunderstorms, and you'll be sheltered from the hail as well.

83 KNOW YOUR LIGHTNING

No two bolts of lightning are the same. Sometimes lightning won't even be a bolt at all. There are a variety of different types of lightning you might encounter.

	INTRA-CLOUD (IC) LIGHTNING	CLOUD-TO-CLOUD (CC) LIGHTNING	CLOUD-TO-GROUND (CG) LIGHTNING	DRY LIGHTNING
RISK TO LIFE	Minimal	Minimal	Severe	Severe
CHARACTERISTICS	A flash of lightning that travels inside a single cloud.	A flash of lightning that travels between two different clouds. Crackling thunder possible.	A brilliant bolt of lightning that extends from clouds to the ground, branching out, forking, and zigzagging along its path.	Cloud-to-ground lightning that occurs in a thunderstorm with little or no precipitation.
DANGERS	The dangers of IC and CC lightning are fairly minimal to most of us mere mortals, but aircraft are frequently (and harmlessly) struck by lightning bolts that occur within and between storm clouds.		Cloud-to-ground lightning can cause damage, fires, and even human and animal injury or death.	Dry lightning is a major problem in grasslands and forests, where it can lead to raging wildfires without rainfall to help put out the flames. It also can pose a risk to humans who might be caught outdoors without safe shelter.

BOLT FROM THE BLUE	"HEAT" LIGHTNING	NEGATIVE LIGHTNING	POSITIVE LIGHTNING	BALL LIGHTNING
Severe	Minimal	Severe	Extreme	Minimal due to its rarity, but there's not enough research to say for sure.
Cloud-to-ground lightning that strikes with no warning, often under clear or blue skies; can come from a thunderstorm 20 or more miles (32 km) away from you.	The phrase "heat lightning" is both popular as well as a misnomer—the term is applied to a thunderstorm that is too distant for you to hear thunder, but you still see flashes in the clouds on the horizon.	Negative lightning is the most common type of lightning that we experience, with the stroke originating from the negatively charged base of a thunderstorm.	The most intense form of lightning, these bolts form from the positively charged regions of the upper thunderstorm. They carry at least 10 times more power than negative lightning and form the majority of bolts from the blue.	Ball lightning is a rare phenomenon that isn't very well understood. Most reports describe ball lightning as a floating orb between the size of an apple and a car lasting several seconds before finally dissipating.
Since people do not usually seek shelter until the storm is on top of them, bolts from the blue are one of the most dangerous types of lightning due to their surprise factor.	Lightning that is far away is generally no cause for concern, but beware of the bolt from the blue.	The risks of negative lightning are the same risks from cloud-to-ground lightning—it can seriously injure or kill you if it strikes you or something nearby. Even if you don't die, the lingering physical side effects of a lightning strike can be debilitating.	Positive bolts of lightning can cause major damage and fires, and are especially lethal if you happen to be struck by one. These very highly energized bolts, while rare, may pose a threat to aircraft as they were discovered and researched after most aircraft safety measures were created.	Eyewitness accounts of ball lightning indicate that it has erratic behavior and can either pass through objects like walls and windows or cause them to burst into flames. Either way, in the unlikely event you encounter ball lightning, it's best that you stay away from it.

84 AVOID LIGHTNING HOT SPOTS

Thunderstorms are prolific lightning producers and they account for almost all of the lightning seen throughout the world. The globe sees more than one billion lightning strikes per year, spread out across almost every single bit of land except for the Arctic and Antarctic Circles, where even the summer air there is usually too cold and stable for thunderstorms to develop.

While the frequent thunderstorms in Florida make it the most lightning-prone region in North America, it's far from the lightning capital of the world. Areas around the equator—where it's fairly hot and humid the whole year—can see thunderstorms almost every day. Venezuela's Lake Maracaibo (pictured above) is noted for its "Catatumbo Lightning," where thunderstorms develop every night near the mouth of the lake for more than half the year, producing an incredible lightning show that can zap the surrounding terrain with hundreds of bolts each night.

The area of the world that sees the highest number of lightning strikes annually is the rainforests and savanna of central Africa, with the most strikes occurring in eastern Democratic Republic of Congo, near the country's border with Uganda and Rwanda. The equatorial areas of Africa, along with the islands of south Asia and the rainforests of South America, are home to the most numerous flashes of lightning on Earth.

85

PREDICT A STRIKE

You can use science to your advantage to know how close a lightning strike is to your location. When you see a flash of lightning, start counting the seconds that elapse between the flash and the clap of thunder. Divide that number by five, and you'll have a rough approximation of how far away the lightning strike occurred, in miles. If you see lightning and count 15 seconds before you hear the thunder, the lightning strike was about 3 miles (5 km) away. It's not precise, but it's a good way to use the speed of sound in a survival situation (or just for fun).

Bottom line? If you can see lightning and hear thunder, you're close enough to be struck. Get indoors as quickly as you can.

86 HELP SOMEONE STRUCK BY LIGHTNING

Contrary to popular belief (and millions of cartoons), lightning victims usually aren't badly burned. You're more likely to end up grappling with these symptoms instead:

A STOPPED HEART The primary cause of death for lightning-strike victims is cardiac arrest. It's also common for the strike to damage the lungs, so a victim may stop breathing. If you know CPR, then chest compressions are the way to go (A).

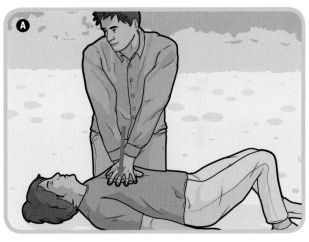

PARALYSIS The victim may not be able to move or speak due to an acute form of paralysis that's unique to lightning strikes—and thankfully temporary. Do your best to keep him or her reassured and warm until medical assistance arrives (B).

MISSING CLOTHES A strike can blow off your clothes. A blanket will help with warmth—and modesty (C).

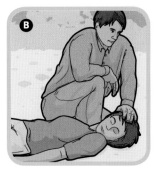

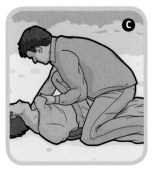

87 SURVIVE A LIGHTNING STRIKE

There are lots of snappy sayings to help you remember lightning safety: *When the thunder roars, go indoors! If you can see it, flee it!* But what do you do when you're caught outdoors with virtually nowhere to hide? The National Outdoor Leadership Schools, or NOLS, and other experts recommend the following.

IF YOU ARE CLOSE TO YOUR VEHICLE OR AN ENCLOSED STRUCTURE Get inside it, no matter what it is—your car, a house, a barn. Open structures such as picnic shelters will provide little to no protection.

IF YOU CANNOT FIND SHELTER Some experts believe that the lightning crouch provides little to no protection from a direct or close strike, but you may feel like any action is better than none. Stand on an insulated pad or bag of clothes. Do not stand on packs; the metal in the frames and zippers could increase chances of a lightning strike. Put your feet together and balance on the balls of your feet. Squat, wrap your arms around your legs, tuck your head, close your eyes, and cover your ears. Maintain the position until danger passes. If you see lightning and

hear thunder, you're close enough to be struck. Get indoors as quickly as you can.

IF YOU ARE CAMPING Avoid open fields and ridge tops during seasons when thunderstorms are prevalent. Stay away from fence lines, metal, and tall, isolated trees. Tents provide no protection. If you are in dangerous open terrain during a thunderstorm, leave the tent and assume the lightning crouch position.

IF YOU ARE IN OPEN COUNTRY Avoid the high ground and contact with dissimilar objects, such as water and land, boulders and land, or single trees and land. Head for ditches, gullies, or low ground. Have your group spread out at least 50 feet (15 m) apart and assume the lightning crouch.

IF YOU ARE ON THE WATER Head inside the boat cabin, which offers a safer environment. Stay off the radio unless it is an emergency. Drop anchor and get as low in the boat as possible. If you're in a canoe on open water, get as low in the canoe as possible and as far as possible from any metal object. If shore only offers rocky crags and tall, isolated trees, stay in the boat.

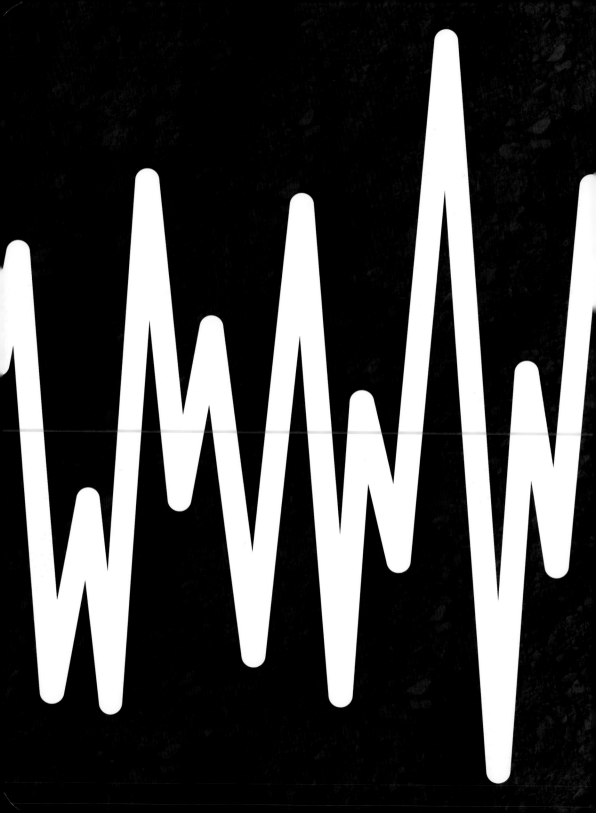

TERRA FIRMA ISN'T ALWAYS SO FIRM.

Avalanches, mudslides, earthquakes, tsunamis, and volcanic eruptions are all earth-shattering examples of nature's ferocious forces coming to bear down on what most of the time is solid ground. Depending on where in the world you live—or where you might travel—you could be exposed to a deluge of snow coming down a mountain, a wall of mud careening down a hillside, seismic shifts or walls of water traveling faster than a jet plane. Buried in your car by snow or mud? Menaced by a tsunami? Caught in the open during a major earthquake? These scary situations are indeed survivable—if you have the right tools and know-how. Here's how to stand strong when the earth shifts mightily under your feet.

88

KNOW YOU'RE IN AVALANCHE COUNTRY

When a layer of snow breaks loose upslope and roars down the mountain at 200 mph (321 km/h), it buries everything in its path. To avoid becoming a human snowball, learn to recognize the danger signs.

WATCH THE WEATHER Avalanche risks increase after a heavy snowfall. The most precarious time of all is when snowy weather is followed by warm weather or rain—and then cold, snowy conditions return.

MEASURE THE SLOPE Most avalanches occur when the slope is 30 to 45 degrees, but even slopes of 25 to 60 degrees can slide if the conditions are right (or, from your perspective, very wrong).

SEEK THE SUN Snow is most volatile on slopes that face away from the sun during winter, so try to plan a route that keeps you off them.

LOOK FOR WRECKAGE Snow debris and broken trees indicate previous avalanches; be wary of these spots.

STEP AROUND MOUNDS Watch out for areas where the wind has piled snow high (especially at the tops of mountains, gullies, and canyons).

RECOGNIZE BAD SNOW Don't tread on snow that makes a hollow sound when you step on it or it looks like large, sparkly crystals instead of fine powder—this is deadly stuff called depth hoar.

BEWARE OF CHUTES Vegetation and boulders act as anchors for snowpack. If there are no trees or rocks on a slope, then it's a big amusement-park slide for snow—and this is one ride you don't want to be on.

WATCH FOR TRIGGERS A loud noise, vibration, or disturbance on the snow caused by snowboarders, skiers, or snowmobiles can trigger avalanches. Be especially cautious when any of these are around.

STAY SAFE Avalanches can strike without warning, so err on the side of safety. If you're hiking, stick to ridgelines, windward hillsides, dense forests, or low-angle slopes. If you're skiing, stay on groomed trails.

89 RECOGNIZE AVALANCHE TYPES

Understanding the conditions that cause avalanches will help you avoid them—and trust me, you definitely want to avoid them.

SLAB AVALANCHES These bad boys account for more than 90 percent of avalanche fatalities. Slab avalanches don't generate from a single point, which might allow a skier or hiker to move laterally out of the way. Instead, an entire sheet of snow—sometimes a massively wide one—gives way at once. Slab avalanches happen when a thick layer of dense snow settles on top of looser snow.

LOOSE-SNOW SLIDES Also called sluffs, these are the least dangerous avalanche types, but they often injure skiers and snowboarders by causing them to change course and head into dangerous terrain. Sluffs occur in cold, dry weather conditions when the snow is powdery and lacks cohesion.

WET AVALANCHES These avalanches tend to move slower than dry avalanches, but they present just as much danger. When temperatures are at or above freezing for a period of days, the surface snow melts and saturates the layers beneath it, making it prone to sliding. To check for wet-avalanche conditions, pick up a handful of snow and squeeze. If your glove gets very wet, it's best to take a different route.

90 ASSESS INCLINE

We all know that most avalanches start on slopes with an angle of 30 to 45 degrees, so these are the ones to avoid at all costs. But how do you figure out the angle on the slope?

If you're an avid mountaineer, you might want to invest in an inclinometer—a reasonably priced tool that measures the slope exactly. If you're not a backcountry hiker, skier, or hunter, that's probably overkill. Instead, tie a small weight to a string (one of the cords on your parka will do), dangle it to touch the snow's surface, and eyeball the slope's angle: A right angle is 90 degrees, so half of that is a dangerous 45-degree angle. If you see that, move it. High-school geometry does come in handy after all.

91 TOTE THE TOOLS

A beacon, probe, and shovel are known as the trinity of avalanche rescue. You'll need all three to rescue people quickly and efficiently, so keep these tools nearby during outings in avalanche country.

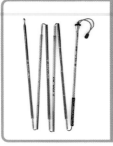

BEACON If you're crazy enough to spend time in areas with unstable snow, you'll definitely need an avalanche beacon. Turn the unit on, set it to transmit, and strap it around your waist and over a shoulder under your outer layer of clothing. Let others know your plans prior to heading out. If you end up buried in the snow, rescuers can pick up your signal and know where to start digging.

PROBE A collapsible probe is a long tool very similar to a tent pole. It's used to feel objects under the avalanche snow (like a buried person), and to focus the excavation effort. It would be impossible to dig up an entire avalanche area in a short amount of time, but a probe coupled with an avalanche beacon can allow rescuers to zero in on a victim's position.

SHOVEL A sturdy shovel is the fastest and safest way to rescue someone buried under the snow, and it allows you to take action pronto, should you encounter a buried victim. Every minute counts in this type of emergency, so the larger the shovel, the more time—and breath, and lives—you'll save.

92 SAVE A SNOW-BURIED VICTIM

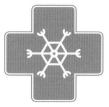

If you are unscathed by an avalanche, but you saw someone go under, you can help him become a survivor.

- Mark the place where you last saw the victim.

- Begin looking for him directly below the last point he was seen above the surface of snow.

- Search the greatest snow deposit first.

- Don't desert anyone trapped under the snow. They may survive for more than an hour.

- Use your phone to call for help. If you cannot call, go for help if you are certain it's only a few minutes away. Mark the route so a rescue party can follow it directly back.

93 BUY A BALLOON

For those who move unprotected through avalanche zones, an avalanche airbag may be the device that saves your life. These airbags are vests or backpacks with a quick-deploying balloon that allows an avalanche victim to stay above the snow, or at least higher in the snow mass. These devices are powered by air, CO2, or nitrogen cylinders, or they are battery operated (you can usually bring the battery-powered units on commercial flights). Though they do not protect a person from the trauma of impacting rocks, ice chunks, or trees, these devices have been shown to save lives. One review found that wearing an avalanche airbag saved an average of 64 out of 100 people who would have otherwise died.

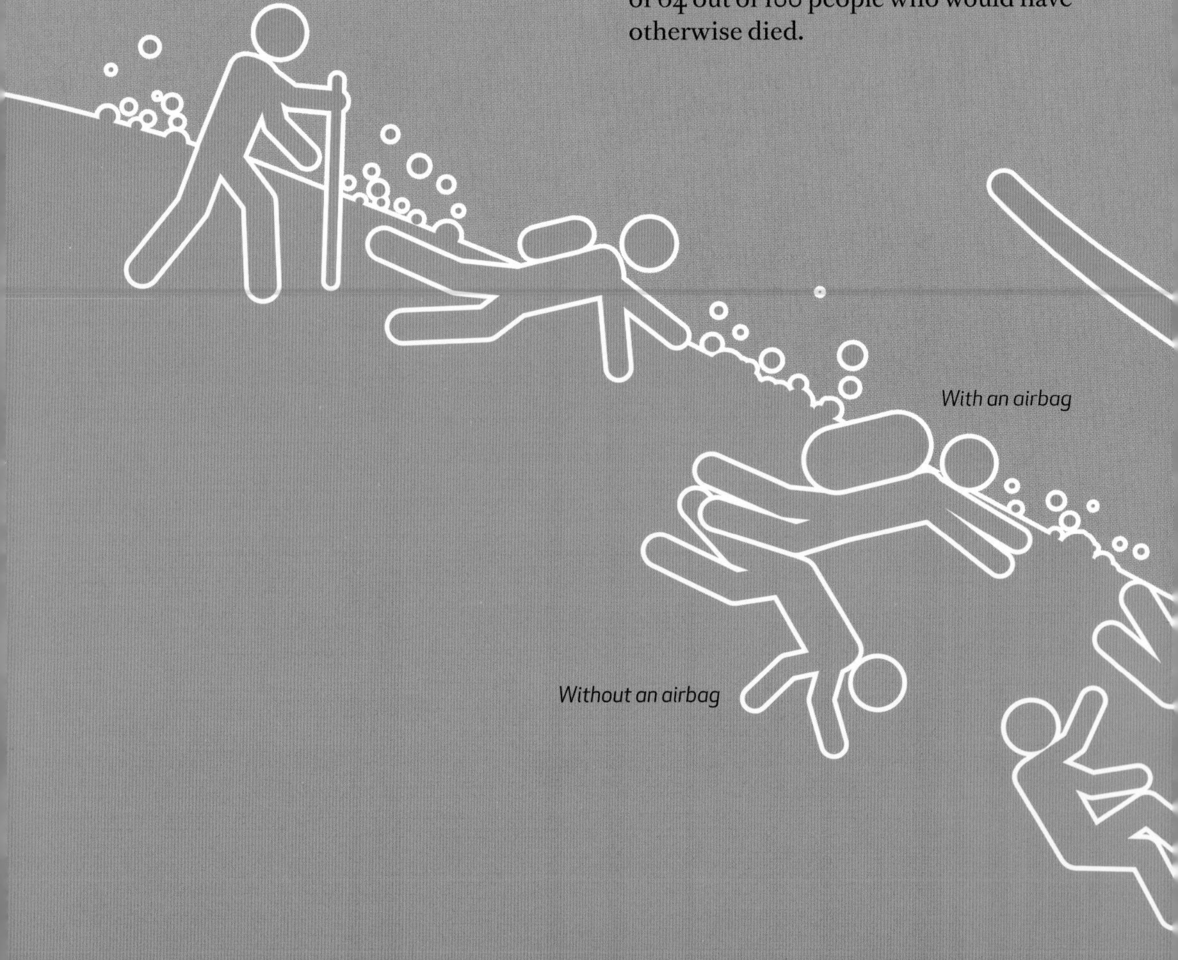

With an airbag

Without an airbag

94 SWIM TO SURVIVE

Snow doesn't exactly move the same way water moves, but there are similarities. If an avalanche breaks loose underfoot, use these techniques to survive.

- Abandon all your equipment. Skis, poles, snowboards, snowshoes, and even snowmobiles will only get in your way or hit you in the churning sea of snow.

- If possible, try to shelter behind rocks, trees, or vehicles. Crouch down and turn your back toward the avalanche.

- If caught out in the open, "swim" through the snow and try to avoid hitting any stationary objects.

- Be aware of dangerous terrain features, like cliffs, boulder fields, groves of trees, or any other hazards.

- As the snow nears you, take a deep breath and cover your nose and mouth.

- Thrust, kick, and swim to stay on the surface. Ride on top of the snow, and attempt to get to the edge of the avalanche.

- Do not yell or open your mouth as the snow hits you, as it can fill your mouth and nose.

- As the avalanche slows, bring your hands and arms up to your face and make an air space so you can breathe.

Flow of avalanche

95 RIDE OUT AN AVALANCHE

Caught in an avalanche? Well, that's plain bad luck. Use skiing (or even surfing) moves to try to ride on top of the snow, and attempt to maneuver toward the edge of the slide. If the snow is moving slowly, try to catch hold of a tree without getting creamed by it. In a fast-moving slide that knocks you off your feet, swim in the snow and try to avoid hitting stationary obstacles.

96 ASSIST YOUR OWN RESCUE

Being buried under the snow is not an enviable position, but it doesn't have to be a fatal one. Once the snow stops moving, it hardens from a fluid into a cementlike consistency. Work quickly to dig your way to the surface as the slide slows. If possible, shove one arm toward the surface and move it around to create an air shaft. Use your hands to carve out a breathing space. Work methodically to avoid exhaustion. Conserve your breath by waiting

to shout until you hear rescuers above you.

If it seems possible to dig yourself out, but you're disoriented from your tumble, you'll need to know which direction is up. If the snow layer above you is relatively thin, daylight might shine through, so go towards that. If you're too deep for light to be your guide, clear a space near your mouth and spit. Watch the direction in which gravity pulls the spit, and head the other way.

SURVIVE IN AN AVALANCHE-BURIED VEHICLE

Getting buried in your vehicle may keep you alive longer than being buried without that protection, but it's still life-threatening. Take these steps to stay alive:

STEP 1 The first and most critical thing to do is turn off the engine. Running the vehicle's engine will not help you melt away your snowy covering, but it will steal your necessary oxygen. Don't smoke or burn any candles while you're buried, either. These activities will waste the precious air that you have.

STEP 2 Partially open a window to find out how deeply you are buried. Use a stick, pole, or gloved hand to see if you can find the snow's surface.

STEP 3 Use your mobile phone, radio, or any communication device to call for assistance.

STEP 4 Don't leave the vehicle if it doesn't seem safe to exit and stay outside. If you feel the snow may collapse on you (if you have to tunnel out) or are in a remote area, create a ventilation tunnel and stay in the car.

98 KNOW WHICH WAY IS UP

You might be able to dig out after an avalanche has tumbled and rolled you—but only if you know which direction is up. If the snow above you is fairly thin, you will see light shining through it—go toward the light. If you're too deep for light to steer you in the right direction, clear a space near your mouth and spit. Watch which way gravity pulls the spit and head the opposite direction.

99 DON'T BURY YOURSELF

Despite the "wisdom" of winter sport movies, the act of yelling or yodeling in the snowy mountains usually doesn't trigger a snowslide. But a good hard wipeout when you're skiing or snowboarding can set off a snow enthusiast-consuming avalanche, and it can even start right beneath your feet. It's true that most avalanche victims trigger the slide that buries them.

This self-activating doom is much less likely to occur on well-traveled ski slopes and trails than in remote environments. In addition to watching out for avalanche-prone areas, watch out for triggers from other outdoor enthusiasts—like that tumble taken by the skier up the slope from your position. And do try to keep your yelling and firecracker-lighting to a minimum.

100

DON'T GET CAUGHT IN A MUDSLIDE

Mudslides occur when sloping ground becomes so saturated with water that the soil loses its grip and gravity takes over. Then you get to deal with a filthy deluge that can destroy your property and put your life at risk. Be smart and heed these warning signs:

KNOW THE STORY Mudslides are recurring events that happen where they've happened before. Contact local authorities to learn the geographical history of your area, including any fires that have destroyed vegetation (which can often lead to soil erosion) or construction that has altered water flow.

AVOID EXTREME INCLINES Steep slopes that are close to the edge of a mountain range or valley are bad news. If you can, simply live somewhere else that's less vulnerable.

WATCH THE WATER Pay attention to changes in the patterns of storm-water drainage on slopes. If there's a river or stream nearby, sudden changes in water level—or a change in color from clear to brown—could indicate an impending slide.

MIND THE GAPS Cracks in pavement or walls pulling away from buildings indicate that the land is moving—which means that it may be vulnerable to mudslides. This is also true if cracks appear in your house's foundation, or if doors and windows start to stick in their frames.

LOOK FOR CROOKED STUFF Any trees or telephone poles that are starting to lean are not charming quirks. They mean the soil is eroding, and you should watch out.

101 RIDE OUT A MUDSLIDE

Mudslides can be spawned by a wide variety of things: heavy storms, earthquakes, volcanic eruptions, or just plain old erosion. However they get their start, they're pretty much always a dirty bad time. Your best survival strategy is to shore up your home against slides before it's too late. Failing that, here are some survival hints:

STAY AWAKE Most mudslide-related deaths occur at night, when people are asleep. If the rain is coming down hard, and flooding and slides are predicted, put on a pot of coffee and continue to monitor weather and evacuation reports.

LISTEN FOR THE RUMBLE Massive amounts of soil, water, and debris don't just come down silently. If you hear a rumbling sound emanating from uphill, evacuate immediately.

GET OUT OF THE SLIDE'S PATH Sometimes there won't be time to evacuate. If you get caught in a mudslide, the best you can do is try to move out of its way. If it's too late for that, curl up into a tight ball and fold your arms over your head for protection.

102 PROTECT YOUR HOME

To prevent your dream home from turning into a muddy nightmare, take these steps to protect yourself and your home:

STEP 1 If you suspect your house may be in a slide zone, have a geological assessment done. Better yet, do that before you buy the home.

STEP 2 Think about the drainage on your property. If your home or yard often floods, use gravity to direct the flow of water away from your foundation. Dig a trench 1 to 2 feet deep (30 cm to 60 cm) and equally wide, and line it with compacted limestone.

STEP 3 Build a vertical retaining wall, which acts as a buffer and prevents land from sliding all the way down a hillside, taking your home with it. A good rule of thumb is to build a system of walls no more than 2 feet (60 cm) in height, staggered down the hillside. Be sure to provide drainage behind the walls, otherwise the soil will erode and then destabilize them.

STEP 4 Topsoil needs some strongly rooted vegetation to keep it in place. Start out with a solid carpeting of sod, followed by trees and a few faster-growing shrubs, such as privets or decorative perennials, such as roses.

103

UNDERSTAND FAULT ACTIVITY

The plates making up our planet's topmost crust are in a constant game of push and shove. Often those plates get stuck together along fault lines, where they store up tension. Eventually, though, something has to give, and the pent-up energy radiates in seismic waves that we feel above ground. That's an earthquake.

An earthquake's magnitude is affected by many factors. In general, the longer the fault line, the larger the quake. Tremors that occur fewer than 43 miles (70 km) underground are deemed "shallow" quakes, and they're more likely to cause dramatic effects on land. There are three main types of faults along which earthquakes occur—and some create worse quakes than others.

What determines an earthquake's intensity? That has much to do with the population density of an affected area, as well as the area's geology: Places with loose soil and rocks are more prone to sliding. Of course, the better a community prepares itself through retrofitting and smart construction, the better off it will be.

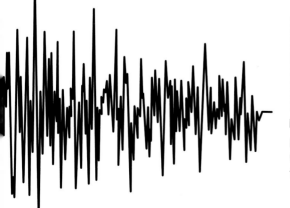

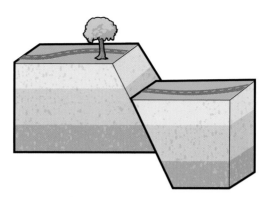

NORMAL FAULTS are also called divergent faults. When pieces of land on opposite sides of a fault pull away from each other, tremors of up to 7.0 magnitude result.

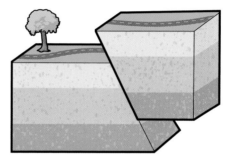

STRIKE-SLIP FAULTS occur where the sides move laterally against each other. Left-lateral faults displace land on the left, while right-lateral faults displace on the right.

REVERSE FAULTS exist where opposite sides push against one another. Reverse faults are the most deadly, creating earthquakes that hit 8.0 on the Richter scale.

104

KNOW EARTHQUAKE HOT SPOTS

Earthquakes—they're just one of the many ways our planet reminds us who's boss. Out of the 500,000 tremors that occur every year, we only feel about 100,000. Every so often, though, one will cause extreme loss of life and structural damage. Luckily, we've been able to identify where in the world such disasters are likely to go down:

PACIFIC RING OF FIRE This is, bar none, the deadliest earthquake territory. More than 80 percent of the world's worst quakes occur on this horseshoe-shape fault system, which stretches up the west side of the Americas, across to Asia, and down into Oceania. Its Liquiñe-Ofqui fault in Chile created the largest earthquake on record—a 9.5 in 1970.

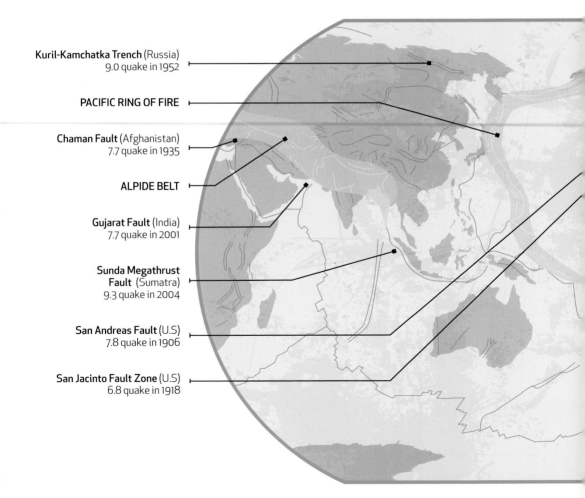

Kuril-Kamchatka Trench (Russia)
9.0 quake in 1952

PACIFIC RING OF FIRE

Chaman Fault (Afghanistan)
7.7 quake in 1935

ALPIDE BELT

Gujarat Fault (India)
7.7 quake in 2001

Sunda Megathrust Fault (Sumatra)
9.3 quake in 2004

San Andreas Fault (U.S)
7.8 quake in 1906

San Jacinto Fault Zone (U.S)
6.8 quake in 1918

ALPIDE BELT This volatile swath of earth extends from Java to Sumatra, up into the Himalayas, and through the Mediterranean into the Atlantic. It's the second most dangerous quake zone in the world and features Turkey's North and East Anatolian faults and the Chaman fault in Afghanistan and Pakistan.

CAYMAN TRENCH This system of fault lines exists between the North American and Caribbean plates, stretching from the Caribbean islands to Guatemala. Here you'll find the Enriquillo-Plantain Garden fault zone, which has caused five major earthquakes in Hispaniola and Jamaica since 1692.

ANYONE'S GUESS Most earthquakes occur where the edges of tectonic plates converge, but some occur well within a plate. These intraplate quakes often cause more damage, as buildings are not retrofitted. Take, for instance, Missouri's New Madrid fault zone, which famously caused 1,000 earthquakes in one year (1811–1812).

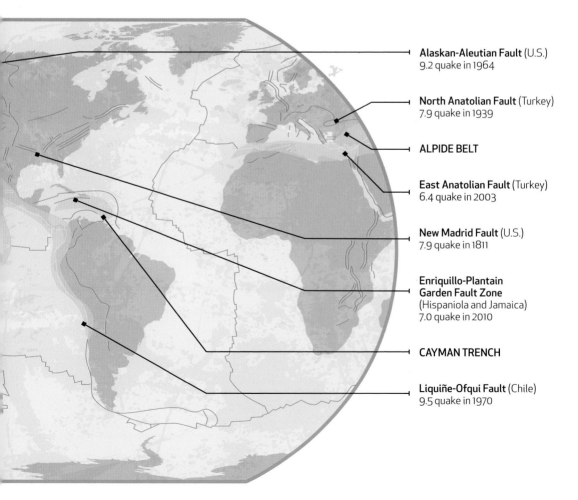

Alaskan-Aleutian Fault (U.S.)
9.2 quake in 1964

North Anatolian Fault (Turkey)
7.9 quake in 1939

ALPIDE BELT

East Anatolian Fault (Turkey)
6.4 quake in 2003

New Madrid Fault (U.S.)
7.9 quake in 1811

Enriquillo-Plantain
Garden Fault Zone
(Hispaniola and Jamaica)
7.0 quake in 2010

CAYMAN TRENCH

Liquiñe-Ofqui Fault (Chile)
9.5 quake in 1970

105

RETROFIT YOUR HOUSE

Live in an area with a lot of seismic activity? Then make sure your house is as close to earthquake-proof as possible by getting it retrofitted. While it's not a guarantee that the Big One won't do a lot of damage, retrofitting helps keep your home anchored to the concrete pad or foundation it's sitting on—even when the earth under it is moving. This task is best left to pros because it's complex and requires expertise.

BOLT IT DOWN Sandwiched between your house and its concrete foundation is a layer of wood called a mudsill. Most likely, your home is already bolted down through this mudsill into the foundation, but in retrofitting, these fasteners are checked and replaced if necessary. Then bolts are added to help keep your house locked down tight.

BRACE THE CRIPPLE WALLS Take a look at your home's foundation. Chances are there's a short wall between the concrete and the floor. This support is called a cripple wall, and it's usually the first thing to collapse in an earthquake, making your home shift dramatically or even fall. You (or your contractor) can reinforce cripple walls by adding plywood panels to both sides of the support.

USE BRACKETS These days, most homes have shear walls, composed of braced panels that resist lateral movement. These are great, but you or the pro you hire might want to reinforce them with angled hold-down brackets. These brackets prevent shear walls from lifting up out of the foundation in a major seismic event.

106

KEEP HOUSEHOLD ITEMS STEADY IN A QUAKE

When there's a whole lot of shakin' going on, there could be a whole lot of falling. And smashing. And crashing. Here's how to keep your home and its contents from tumbling down around or on you in an earthquake. (All the items mentioned here are readily available in hardware stores.)

BATTEN DOWN THE BIG STUFF Strap water heaters to the wall with perforated metal strips known as plumber's tape. Make sure that all piping is flexible rather than rigid, and insert a nonflammable spacer between the heater and the wall. For refrigerators and large appliances, use an L-bracket to bolt the top to the wall. To secure your fridge's bottom to the floor, use pronged Z-clips.

MAKE SURE FURNITURE IS FIXED IN PLACE Secure large objects such as cabinets, bookcases, and hutches to the wall using L-brackets or furniture-securing kits. Equip all cabinets with latches to keep their contents from spilling out.

STOP THE SHATTERING Apply clear polyester sheets to help keep windows and mirrors from breaking. You can find them at a home-supply store.

BEWARE OF WALL HANGINGS Place heavier ornamental items like mirrors or paintings only on walls well away from beds and seating areas. Don't count on a hook and nail to hold them in place—use wall anchors instead.

REARRANGE DISPLAYS Move heavy objects to lower shelves so they'll do less damage if they're shaken loose. Place objects with low centers of gravity, like fishbowls and vases, on nonstick mats to help keep them in place.

SWEAT THE SMALL STUFF Apply earthquake putty to the bottom of small items so they won't move.

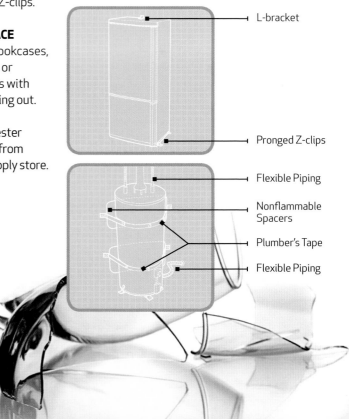

L-bracket

Pronged Z-clips

Flexible Piping

Nonflammable Spacers

Plumber's Tape

Flexible Piping

107

RIDE OUT AN EARTHQUAKE

When an earthquake strikes, the immediate priority is to get to a safe place to ride out the tremblor, but where you are at the time will determine what you do next.

If you are indoors when the earthquake begins, drop to your hands and knees and cover your head and neck with your arms. Move under any additional cover, such as under a sturdy desk or table, if you need to take shelter from the danger of falling objects. Stay away from glass, windows, outside doors and walls, or anything that could fall, such as items on shelves or furniture. Wait and remain inside until the shaking stops. Avoid doorways, as they do not provide protection from falling or flying objects.

If you are awakened by an earthquake, remain in bed and cover your head and neck with a pillow. Moving in the dark may result in more injuries than remaining in bed, as you won't be able to see debris or hazards, or judge how safe it is to move.

Should you be outdoors, get to open space if possible. Move away from buildings, streetlights, and utility wires. If you're in a dense urban area such as downtown in a city, you may be at less risk from falling debris if you get inside. Once you reach a safe spot, drop to your hands and knees and hold on until the quake stops.

If you're driving when an earthquake occurs, stop as quickly and safely as possible. Remain in the vehicle; avoid stopping near or under buildings, trees, overpasses, and utility wires. Proceed carefully once the earthquake has stopped, but be aware of aftershocks. Avoid underpasses, bridges, or ramps that the earthquake may have damaged.

108 DRIVE IN A QUAKE

You probably know the drill: If you're inside a building when an earthquake hits, stay there. If you're outside, get into a clearing. But what if you're driving?

STOP FOR THE SHAKING There are two hazards if an earthquake strikes when you're driving: other drivers and falling objects. Pull over in an area free of things that might fall on your car, such as telephone poles, street lights, and, yes, even overpasses. The more open the area, the safer it is.

DEAL WITH INFRASTRUCTURE If you're on a bridge, take the next exit off it. And if you're stuck under that overpass, get out of your car and lie flat beside it. Should the structure collapse, it will crush your car, but not to the ground—which will hopefully leave a safe zone immediately surrounding the vehicle.

HEAD HOME There may be aftershocks, so don't hurry off. Listen to the radio for updates that may affect your route, and expect accidents and damage.

109

SURVIVE UNDER DEBRIS

The saying "earthquakes don't kill people, buildings do" reminds us of the risk of being trapped under debris or in a collapsed structure. If you survive an earthquake but end up trapped, you must be prepared to survive on your own with limited resources and space until rescuers can reach you. In order to improve your chances of survival, here are some important tips.

KEEP IN TOUCH If you have your phone, try calling, texting, or posting to social media. If none of those works, there may be an outage in the area. Turn your phone off to conserve the battery and try again every few hours.

DOUSE FLAMES Don't use a match or lighter to see where you are, as there could be a risk of explosion from gas leaks.

BREATHE EASY As dust settles from the collapse, cover your mouth and nose with a cloth. Avoid any movement that kicks up more dust, as that continues to make breathing more difficult.

SIGNAL FOR HELP You can call for help by tapping on a pipe or wall. If you have a whistle, use it instead of your voice, as yelling will tire you very quickly.

CONSERVE SUPPLIES If you have any food or drink on your person or accessible in the void, ration it carefully; you don't know how long you'll need it to last.

110 ASSESS A CONCUSSION

Concussions are common head injuries caused by a variety of circumstances, including car accidents, sports, a fall, or a blow to the head from falling debris.

Begin by checking to see if the victim has a bleeding head injury. If so, bandage the injury, but it's still common for concussions to develop localized swelling, or a "goose egg." Either way, visible external injuries are not a good gauge of severity, as even minor scalp wounds can have profuse bleeding.

Have the person lie down and rest. Place a cold compress (frozen peas, cold pack, or ice, wrapped in a towel) on their head, and monitor them for the next 24 hours to ensure they haven't gotten worse. Most symptoms of a concussion will resolve on their own, but if they persist or worsen, or if there are other serious signs, such as slurred speech, seizures, prolonged unconsciousness, or blood or clear fluid coming from their ears or nose, call for an ambulance and get medical help immediately.

You should look for the following signs and symptoms:

- Balance problems or dizziness
- Drowsiness or feeling sluggish
- Confusion or brief loss of consciousness
- Drowsiness or feeling sluggish
- Double vision or blurred vision
- Headache
- Nausea or vomiting
- Sensitivity to light or noise

111 TAKE ACTION AFTER AN EARTHQUAKE

Surviving the shake doesn't mean you're out of the woods. What you do immediately after an earthquake is just as important as what you do during one.

PREVENT FIRE If the building you're in appears to be structurally sound, open doors and windows to ventilate gas fumes or dust. Avoid using any gas or electrical appliances, because the greatest danger after an earthquake is fire.

PROTECT YOURSELF Before you go running out into the street, put on boots or shoes with heavy soles, and find a pair of sturdy gloves to wear. Both will help you avoid dangers you can't necessarily see—such as sharp objects and electrical hazards.

MAKE AN ESCAPE If you're leaving a multistory building, be aware that stairwells may shift. Descend slowly so you can be sure of your footing, and don't run: It could disturb and weaken the stairs even further.

KNOW TSUNAMI WARNING SIGNS

A tsunami can travel through deep water at more than 600 mph (965 km/h), crossing an ocean in less than a day. And it won't calm down when it hits shore: Shallower water actually makes it taller. Here's how to tell if a big wave is headed your way.

A MAJOR SHAKE-UP An earthquake in a coastal region is an obvious sign. If you live near the earthquake, seek higher ground. Even if the quake is across the ocean, monitor broadcasts—tsunamis travel long distances.

ANTSY ANIMALS Look out for changes in animal behavior—both pets and livestock. Scientists believe critters pick up on the Earth's vibrations before we do, so if they're nervous, it may be for good reason.

RECEDING WATER The first part of a tsunami to reach land is the drawback trough, which causes coastal waters to recede, exposing normally submerged areas. If you spot a drawback, you've got about five minutes before the big wave hits.

113 DEAL WITH A TSUNAMI AT SEA

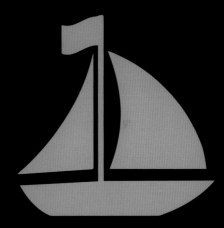

One of the safest places to be during an earthquake-triggered tsunami is on a boat in deep water. A quake beneath the ocean floor produces a powerful energy impulse that races horizontally through the water, but in the deep ocean that energy flows through without disturbing the surface. When that energy meets the shallows, the water rises up into a wave.

If you're on a boat in a harbor and you learn that a tsunami is coming, either immediately head for deeper water or abandon the boat and get to high ground. If you're on your way to deep water and the first wave catches you, steer the boat up the wave and apply maximum throttle to climb the swell. Keep heading for deeper water until the entire event has passed.

114

BRACE FOR A BIG WAVE

Earthquakes are not the only cause of tsunamis. In fact, volcanic activity, landslides, or impact from space objects can all set one off. Large tsunami waves can sweep inland to elevations as high as 100 feet (30 m), so you'll want to get at least that high above sea level. Whenever you're in a coastal area, think of where to go in a big-wave emergency.

PLOT YOUR ESCAPE Do a little recon to identify escape routes to high ground. Plan on following designated tsunami evacuation routes (if they're established in your area) or simply heading inland and uphill as quickly as possible.

STAY TUNED Keep your ear tuned to the radio and TV for warnings. Evacuate immediately upon receiving news of an impending tsunami.

GET THE HECK OUT Don't go to the beach to watch the big waves. Meet up with your loved ones as quick as you can and head for high ground.

115 SURVIVE BEING SWEPT AWAY IN A TSUNAMI

Getting caught up in a tsunami is like being trapped in a raging river with rapids and falls—only worse. You're caught in a wild maelstrom, along with a floating junkyard full of jagged metal, nail-studded lumber, raw sewage, twisted vehicles, panic-stricken animals, and dead bodies. How are you ever going to survive that?

AVOID THE FACE The greatest force of a wave is in its breaking face. This churning mass also carries the majority of pulverizing debris. If you're going to get swept away, at least try to hold on to something secure until this deadly part of the wave passes.

SCRAMBLE TO THE TOP After the dreaded face, there'll be several waves. With them come the thing that makes tsunamis deadly and the thing that gives you a fighting chance: debris, and lots of it. Fight and claw your way on top of anything that floats and cling to it for dear life. If the next wave gets higher than the first wave, drag yourself to a higher point.

GET BACK TO LAND In a tsunami, you're either going inland with the initial surge or being dragged out to sea. If it's the latter, keep the shore in sight and swim parallel to it as you would do to escape a rip current. Float as much as possible, and use energy-efficient strokes like the backstroke to get back to solid ground.

116

SURVIVE A VOLCANIC ERUPTION

When the earth blows its top, the dangers include fiery lava bombs lobbed by the eruption, a tide of molten rock, and the toxic fumes of pyroclastic gas flows.

HIT THE ROAD, JACK The best place to be is far away. Distance is the best protection against the hellfire and fury of a volcano, so be ready to evacuate when the warning is issued.

TAKE SHELTER If you can't put space between you and the eruption, find shelter and cross your fingers. A house can provide protection from ash and falling debris, but then again, it could catch on fire. So if you shelter inside, be ready to hustle out fast. Taking shelter inside a vehicle also might protect against some dangers. Since things that flow go downhill, wherever you hole up, make sure it's not in a low-lying area.

117
BEWARE OF VOLCANIC HAZARDS

Movies have typically portrayed red-hot lava as the biggest danger during an eruption, but there are really many more different types of potential hazards from volcanic activity, and lava is the least dangerous of them.

Molten rock usually flows relatively slowly, but lava is only the most commonly known part of an eruption. Along with lava, volcanoes will also eject other fallout—there are various pyroclastic materials, ranging in size from fragments to giant rocks, that can be thrown a short distance or ejected into the upper atmosphere. Volcanoes also release hot gases that produce acid rain and air pollution that can spread far on wind currents, affecting regional or global climate.

In an eruption, water, debris, ash, and other materials can combine into a heavy slurry that can move quickly and with destructive force. The heat from the eruption can melt snowpack or divert rivers or streams, leading to flash floods. An erupting volcano also can trigger landslides, avalanches, earthquakes, and tsunamis.

After an eruption, seek a reliable source of emergency information to determine which hazards you may be facing, and respond accordingly. Prepare to evacuate the area; avoid spots downwind and river valleys downstream of the volcano.

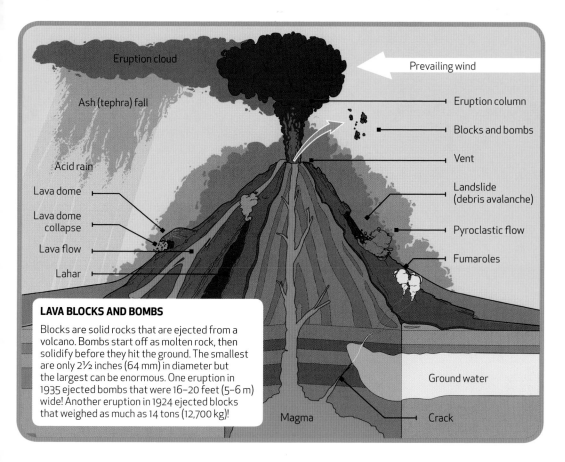

Eruption cloud

Ash (tephra) fall

Prevailing wind

Eruption column

Blocks and bombs

Vent

Acid rain

Lava dome

Landslide (debris avalanche)

Lava dome collapse

Pyroclastic flow

Lava flow

Fumaroles

Lahar

Ground water

Magma

Crack

LAVA BLOCKS AND BOMBS

Blocks are solid rocks that are ejected from a volcano. Bombs start off as molten rock, then solidify before they hit the ground. The smallest are only 2½ inches (64 mm) in diameter but the largest can be enormous. One eruption in 1935 ejected bombs that were 16–20 feet (5–6 m) wide! Another eruption in 1924 ejected blocks that weighed as much as 14 tons (12,700 kg)!

118 COPE WITH ASH

Volcanic ash isn't soft and fluffy—as if the mountain had been in a pillow fight. Nope, ash is composed of tiny jagged pieces of rock and glass: hard, abrasive, and corrosive. Because it destroys engines when it's sucked into the intake, volcanic ash can halt air travel and hamper ground transportation for hundreds of miles around an eruption. But if you live close to an active volcano, your problems might be more immediate.

TAKE COVER During ash fall, stay inside—especially if you have a respiratory ailment. Close doors, windows, vents, and chimney flues. Monitor radio and TV broadcasts about the situation.

WEAR LAYERS When outside, wear long sleeves and pants. Breathe through a dust mask, or hold a damp cloth over your nose and mouth. Use goggles or wear eyeglasses instead of contact lenses.

START SHOVELING Ash accumulations can pile deep on roofs, requiring shovel work to prevent them from collapsing. Make sure you clear rain gutters as well.

BE CAREFUL ON THE ROAD To prevent engine damage, avoid driving. If you must, keep your speed down and bear in mind that some roads may be impassable until snowplows clear them.

119 LOOK OUT FOR LAHAR

"Lahar" is originally an Indonesian term used to describe the mixture of material and water that flows down the slopes of a volcano or valley. A lahar is said to look like a moving mass of wet concrete that carries debris, rocks, and even large boulders.

Lahars can vary in size, speed, and danger. Large lahars can be thousands of feet wide and hundreds of feet tall. The most dangerous ones flow much faster than humans can run, up to 60 mph (100 km/h), and can flow for hundreds of miles before finally coming to rest.

120

ASSESS A LAVA FIELD

Even if you're pretty sure it has cooled and hardened, it's better to detour around a lava field—because if you're wrong, you're toast. Literally.

TREAD LIGHTLY If you must cross, try to ensure that the lava has totally hardened. You can't always tell from looking because molten lava might be flowing below a thin crust that can fool you. As you make your way forward, probe the ground ahead with a stick.

DO A SNIFF TEST Pay attention to air quality. Sulfur dioxide gases indicate flowing lava beneath you. This gives you two reasons to get away: Not only is the ground unstable, but also that gas is toxic.

HEED YOUR FEET If the soles of your boots start to melt, that's a very bad sign: The flow is too hot to cross. And if the ground feels at all mushy, that means it's too unstable to cross—and you definitely want to take that detour.

HOT AND
BOTHERED

WHEN THE HEAT IS ON, STAY COOL.

The very thing that keeps us warm in the winter—the heat blasting from a furnace or the flames of a roaring fire—can, in uncontrolled circumstances, be miserable and deadly. Whether it shows up in the form of a house fire, wildfire, killer heat wave, soil-parching drought, or a scorching desert sandstorm, here are strategies for putting it out—or getting out—in order to keep you and your family safe. The game plan could be as simple as collecting rainwater to keep the vegetable garden growing during a drought—or as drastic as outrunning a wind-whipped wildfire, but with preparation and improvisation, you can escape the heat without so much as getting singed.

121

RIDE THE WAVE

The exact threshold for a heat wave differs from country to country, but in the United States, the National Weather Service defines a heat wave as a period of two or more days with excessively high temperatures.

Most heat waves are caused by strong ridges of high pressure parking over a region for an extended period of time, allowing calm conditions and sunny skies to gradually bake the area. One infamous cause of heat waves in the United States and Canada is known as the ring of fire, or a strong high pressure that sets up over the central United States, allowing blazing

temperatures and choking humidity to blanket the area for a week or longer, in some cases.

Weather conditions that constitute a heat wave are pretty relative around the world. Europe and western Asia can see death tolls in the hundreds after a heat wave that seems mild compared to what other parts of the world experience—many homes in places like Italy or Russia are not equipped with air conditioners, so residents who are already not accustomed to warmer-than-normal temperatures can succumb to heat pretty quickly during a sustained heat wave.

122 STAY CHILL

High temperatures can be worse than insufferable: They can be deadly. To make matters worse, everyone using their air conditioners at once can trigger a power outage. And if you thought a heat wave wasn't fun, try a heat wave without air conditioning. Here's what to do when the mercury rises:

BE SUN SAVVY Open windows on the shaded side of the house. On the sunny side of the house, hang exterior shades to block the intense sun from hitting windows.

PROMOTE CIRCULATION Open the doors and set battery-operated box fans in each entry. They'll expel hot air while drawing cooler air inside.

STAY LOW Remember the old adage about hot air rising? Now's the time that information comes in handy. Keep to your home's lowest level, where the air is coolest.

GET WET Soak your feet in a basin of water, and wear a damp bandanna around your head. If you have one, fill a spray bottle with water and give yourself a cooling spritz every so often.

DRINK UP Make sure you're getting lots of water, and slow down to reduce perspiration and overheating. Avoid caffeine or alcohol, as they'll just dehydrate you.

UNPLUG IT If your power is on, know that all your household appliances create heat—and that heat really adds up. Unplug computers and lamps with incandescent bulbs, and make meals that don't require heat-generating appliances, such as stoves.

123 SURVIVE HEAT ILLNESS

There's heat, and then there's extreme heat—the kind that skyrockets your core body temperature, making you dizzy and hot to the touch. In severe circumstances, heat illness can even be fatal.

HEAT EXHAUSTION The milder of the two heat-related ailments, heat exhaustion occurs when the body's temperature gets too high. People affected experience dizziness, nausea, fatigue, heavy sweating, and clammy skin. The treatment is simple: Have the victim lie down in the shade, elevate his or her feet, and supply plenty of fluids.

HEATSTROKE If a person's core body temperature reaches 104° F (40°C), he or she needs immediate treatment for heatstroke, which can be deadly. Besides an alarming thermometer reading, the easiest signs to identify are hot, dry skin; headache; dizziness; and unconsciousness. Heatstroke is life-threatening and requires immediate treatment in a hospital, as it can damage the kidneys, brain, and heart if it goes on for too long at too high a temperature. For transport to the hospital, or if you're waiting for medics, elevate the victim's head and wrap him or her in a wet sheet.

124 WATCH OUT FOR CITY HEAT

We've all made this mistake—it's a slow summer afternoon and you're expecting something important in the mail. You're too lazy to throw your shoes on, and the mailbox is right there. You do what any other red-blooded human would do and make a run for it. You realize your mistake the moment your feet hit the pavement, but it's too late. You can almost hear the sizzle of your foot cooking beneath you.

It's a painful reminder that some surfaces retain heat better than others. Asphalt and concrete warm up much faster than surfaces like mulch and grass, so their temperature (and that of the air just above them) is often much, much hotter than their surroundings. As your feet have surely found out, it's no small difference.

Now, imagine that happening over the entire expanse of a bustling city—all of those cars, hot roofs, brick and concrete facades, and endless sidewalks and asphalt roadways, snaking their way from one end of town to the other. These surfaces allow a considerable amount of heat to build up, and it culminates in a very real phenomenon known as the "urban heat island."

The urban heat island effect is a well-documented occurrence seen in most cities (small and large), causing downtown areas to get as much as 5–10% hotter than the surrounding suburbs. Beyond all of the problems it can cause in recording weather observations, there's a hidden health hazard in this artificial heat.

City centers are often home to a large number of elderly and impoverished citizens, many of whom can't afford simple cooling devices like fans or air conditioning. When a particularly brutal heat wave hits, the urban heat island effect can injure or kill a disproportionate number of people who live in cities, compared to residents of the surrounding areas.

LINE IT UP

Mesoscale convective systems (MCS) often form from clusters of thunderstorms that develop close to one another, such as pop-up thunderstorms or even supercells. If these storms are close enough to each other and in a favorable environment, their cold pools (the rain-cooled air that descends to the surface) can merge together, allowing the thunderstorms to organize into a line.

DEADLY LINEUP This large, unified cold pool can start rolling across the landscape with thunderstorms following closely behind. The cold pool looks like an invisible bubble, and as it collides with the warm and humid atmosphere in front of it, it forces the unstable air to rise into the storms along its leading edge. This upward motion of unstable air becomes the updraft for the line of storms, allowing them to survive and thrive for as long as the inflow of warm air continues unimpeded.

WICKED WINDS The biggest feature of a mesoscale convective system is the destructive winds it can produce. As the cold pool rushes along the surface, air behind the storms in the pool itself will start rotating vertically, sort of like a wheel rolling across the ground. This rotating air can cause a jet of winds in the midlevels of the atmosphere called a "rear inflow jet"—these winds rush toward the storms from behind, only to collide with the thunderstorms' downdrafts and careen groundward, producing winds at the surface of more than 100 mph (160 km/h) at times.

HOURS OF RAIN Under favorable conditions, a mesoscale convective system can last an impressively long time, surviving for more than a day and traveling thousands of miles from where it began. One of these wind machines won't die out until the cold pool moves too far ahead of the storms to allow air to continue rising or the line of storms runs into stable air, starving the storms of energy.

126

DEAL WITH A DROUGHT

Drought is simply an absence of moisture when below-average rainfall depletes water stores and dries up wells. There's no specific moment at which a dry spell becomes a drought. Some droughts have been declared after just a couple of weeks. What matters most is how long droughts last. In normal circumstances, a drought can last for a few months to a year. But more extreme droughts, such as the one in California that began in 2012, can last years before the cycle is broken.

HAVE A PLAN Developed countries are typically sheltered from the deleterious effects of droughts, notably loss of food and drinking water. These countries typically have reserves and food options available that render the drought's effects moot unless you live or work in an industry that is water dependent. Farmers and ranchers have to plan ahead in ways average citizens do not. Similarly, city governments and municipalities have to have a water-conservation plan, which may include taking water-intensive farmlands out of rotation to keep the water for residents.

SEE IT COMING The key to drought management is recognizing the conditions in their early stages. While droughts can't be effectively predicted yet, historical data illustrates that they will happen and happen often. As a result, governments monitor not only rainfall but also peripheral conditions like snowpack, water tables, reservoir levels, and humidity trends. Additional factors such as extended periods of high heat or wind—which dries out soil—also can exacerbate the conditions that lead to a drought. Monitoring all these factors helps governments recognize droughts and act accordingly.

CATCH YOUR RAIN

A lot of people hear "rain catchment" and think of a system that is either too large to be practical or too complicated to DIY. Here's a quick and easy way to grab the rain. It's an afternoon project that can have a huge impact in a drought, for watering a vegetable garden or for flushing toilets. Do note that you'll have even more success with this system if you have a roofline within a gutter. Also, make sure it's legal in your area.

STEP 1 Make a trough by screwing three deck boards together—one as the base and two for the sides. Use a clear, silicone sealer along the seams to keep the water from leaking out. When choosing your wood, avoid synthetics and pressure-treated lumber.

STEP 2 Buy a handful of containers (the number will depend on the size of your rain trough) suitable for storing water. Choose containers that have a 2-inch (5 cm) opening.

STEP 3 Line up your containers under the trough. Remember that containers expand when filled with water, so leave a little space between them. Then use a hole saw attached to a power drill to cut holes in the bottom of the trough.

STEP 4 Cut 6-inch (15 cm) lengths of PVC pipe that fit in the holes in the bottom of your trough. Then use PVC narrowing conduits at the top of each length. Use a miter saw to cut out a small area of the conduit where it sits on the trough. This cutout will help funnel rainwater directly into your containers. You also can drill several holes of substantial diameter to achieve the same end.

STEP 5 Drop the pipe/conduit into the trough cutouts and into the container openings. Putting more silicone sealer around the base will help keep you from losing water.

Once you've got your system set up, you can fashion some simple legs to attach to the end. Then just set up your trough and wait for it to rain.

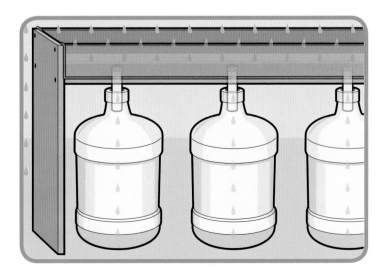

128

SURVIVE A SANDSTORM

"Haboob" is the Arabic word for a sandstorm, a massive cloud of sand and dust that can overtake a city and drop visibility to nothing for long periods of time.

STORM CHASERS These impressive and dangerous phenomena are pretty common in and around desert areas, especially during the storm season when gusty winds are likely. Most develop on the edges of storms that sweep through a desert. Strong winds can dig up the loose top layer of sediment from the desert floor, lofting it into the atmosphere and carrying it hundreds or thousands of miles from its original location.

DUST DEVILS Dust storms make daily life extremely difficult; these events are responsible for countless traffic fatalities around the world, not to mention thousands of medical emergencies from dust and sand aggravating respiratory conditions. Some of the largest haboobs on Earth sweep off of the Sahara Desert and into the Atlantic Ocean, sometimes reaching the shores of North America as dust high in the upper atmosphere. This dust is often accompanied by extremely dry air, which can affect weather around the world.

SURVIVAL TIPS Always have goggles and a mask, or at least a bandana, handy if you're going to be traveling in areas where sandstorms are likely. If you're in a vehicle, and the storm is at a reasonable distance, you may be able to outrun it. Otherwise, stop and ride it out in your car. If you are not in a vehicle and no shelter is near, all you can do is lie down and ride out the storm. Get to higher ground if possible. Not surprisingly, the blowing sand is most concentrated close to the ground. Cover your head with your arms or a backpack to protect against any objects being hurled by the wind.

129 DRIVE IN A SANDSTORM

Sand may not seem especially scary, but when the wind lifts it 50 feet (15 m) into the air and propels it at 75 mph (120 km/h), it suddenly seems a lot fiercer than it does when you're at the beach. If you're on the road when a sandstorm hits, here are your options:

STOP If you observe dense sand blowing across the highway ahead, stop and wait for it to pass. But don't just halt in the middle of the pavement, as visibility is compromised in a sandstorm. Pull off the road as far as possible,

turn off your lights, set the emergency brake, and take your foot off the brake pedal. This way, other drivers won't follow your lights and crash into you.

KEEP GOING If leaving the pavement is dangerous because of a drop-off or other obstacle, turn on your headlights, sound the horn periodically, and drive at a slow speed. Stay alert for other drivers doing the same. Don't turn off the road you're on, as it's easy to become disoriented in such low visibility.

LET IT BURN (SAFELY)

The very element that sparked the advancement and survival of humankind is able to take it away in one swift instant. Fire is a terrifying and powerful force that shows no mercy to anything in its path. Much safety education around the world is devoted to preventing and dealing with the scourge of fire. The majority of blazes that occur in our homes and vehicles are easily preventable, but the flames that can reduce the land to ash aren't always so easy to stop.

Wildfires can burn a small patch of grass or huge expanses of forest, eliminating hundreds of years of growth and clouding the sky with so much billowing smoke that people in another country are affected by the burned remains of another's former beauty.

Some fires are more dangerous than others—most burn harmlessly out in the middle of nowhere, threatening few or no humans, while a few can threaten heavily populated cities or produce choking, toxic smoke that can injure or kill people thousands of miles away.

Fires are nature's way of cleaning up the place—almost all of the fires that occur in the wild are sparked by lightning, burning the dead matter and underbrush that crowds the ground and stifles new growth. Wildfires are a natural and healthy part of the environment's life cycle, but as humanity grew and expanded into previously uninhabited lands, even small blazes became a life-threatening nuisance.

It contradicts everything we were taught as children, but those fire-safety messages from the likes of that preachy, anthropomorphic bear have been too effective—we're so good at preventing even small fires that forests and wooded areas are wildly overgrown, so much so that tiny fires can blow up into monsters that engulf huge expanses of real estate and threaten more people than they would have otherwise.

It may be counter-intuitive, but one of the best ways we can recognize the hazards of wildfires and survive them in the future is to realize that we need to let some fires burn. Some buildings and habitats will be destroyed in the process, but it's a natural part of the environment, and disrupting the trend would prove more disastrous and deadly in the long run.

131 PREDICT A FIRE

Meteorologists can use forecast models and observations to predict when the right combination of heat, humidity, wind, and other variables like vegetation moisture will create dangerous fire weather in any particular location. The National Weather Service issues red flag warnings when weather conditions could lead to the rapid formation and spread of fires. Here are the four major conditions that can prime an environment to go up in smoke:

HEAT It seems like heat would be the most important variable, but all heat does is allow the relative humidity to drop dangerously low. Hot summer days in a dry atmosphere can drive relative humidity down to 10 percent or lower, allowing vegetation to dry up like jerky and give fires the fuel they need to rage.

HUMIDITY Relative humidity is "relative" because it measures the amount of moisture in the air when you take into account both dew point and air temperature. When they're close together, relative humidity is high, and when they're far apart, there's very low relative humidity. We've all experienced those days when our skin dries out in an instant—just imagine what those extremely low humidity levels do to plants. Days with low relative humidity can easily suck the moisture out of vegetation, making it an easy target for fire to consume.

WIND The wind plays a critical role in whether a fire remains localized or spreads into an epic inferno. Winds as low as 15 mph (24 km/h) are sufficient to transport sparks to surrounding fuel, allowing a small campfire to spread to neighboring trees, turning into a blaze that firefighters struggle for weeks to control.

STORMS Not all thunderstorms are accompanied by precipitation. Many drier climates are plagued by a phenomenon known as "dry thunderstorms" during the warm season. These storms produce little or no precipitation, allowing lightning to strike dried-out vegetation with no rain to extinguish the flames. Lightning produced by dry thunderstorms is responsible for some of the worst fires in the western United States.

PREPARE

PHONE Program the direct dial number for your fire department into your cell phone.

ESCAPE If your building doesn't have a fire escape, have folding escape ladders available.

NETWORK Connect your fire alarm to central monitoring (can be tied in with your burglar alarm). Network all your smoke alarms together for simultaneous alarm.

SPRINKLERS Get a sprinkler system installed.

EXTINGUISH Keep a fire extinguisher on hand.

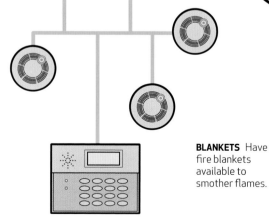

BLANKETS Have fire blankets available to smother flames.

If a fire should break out in or near your home, it pays to be well prepared with multiple methods of putting out the fire (and different kinds of fires can call for different methods of extinguishing them) or getting away from it.

Even if you don't have a full firefighting plan for your home—or if you are somewhere that lacks the resources—you can still deal with fires if you act quickly using tools you have on hand.

IMPROVISE

BAKING SODA Apply baking soda to grease fires.

EXTINGUISH Use a garden hose, a bucket of water or sand, or a shovel and dirt to extinguish the fire.

BREATHE Breathe though a wet handkerchief.

ESCAPE Climb out of a window using sheets and/or rope tied together.

PHONE Dial 911 on your cell phone.

133 FIRESCAPE YOUR HOME

Homeowners in fire-prone areas have long understood that prevention really does go a long way. But you can use these tips in any area, even in cities, to help keep your home safe. Clearing the area around your home can make the difference between simply surviving a wildfire, and surviving it with a home to return to.

On your house itself, keep ⅛-inch (3 mm) mesh over all vent coverings to prevent embers from entering the attic or other spaces. And be sure to use fire-retardant tiles and materials where possible on the roof and other walls.

Try dividing your property into four zones, then prepare each zone accordingly. None of this is a guarantee that your home will make it through unscathed, but it can tip the odds in your favor.

ZONE 1 Mark out an area 30 feet (9 m) around your home. This is the critical zone. Don't allow any tall plants or trees in this area. Instead, if you keep a lawn, keep it low, well-irrigated, and green. Resist those pretty bushes and tall flowers up against your house. Instead, keep it open. Even in the city, this space will allow fire vehicles access to any location they need to reach.

ZONE 2 Within that 30-foot (9 m) buffer, but away from the house, go with drought-tolerant plants. A drip irrigation system in this zone also will keep the soil moist and the plants healthy and less prone to fire damage.

ZONE 3 In choosing to plant trees (or leave them standing), think about height. Pick species that are a little lower, underneath that 30-foot (9 m) height, so if they fall, they won't fall on any structures. Low-growing, drought-resistant plants also function as better ground cover. If the low vegetation catches fire, you want to keep upward and outward sparks at a minimum. Do not plant conifers—they can virtually explode in high heat.

ZONE 4 This is the safe zone farthest away from your house. Don't allow your home to transition straight from manicured to wild, however. You don't have to do a ton of work here, but keep the ground cover knocked down, and clear out any dead vegetation.

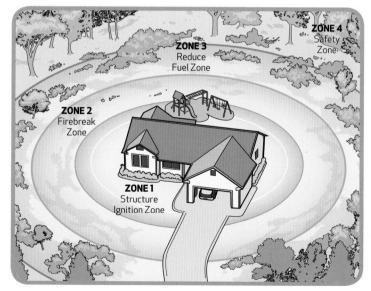

ZONE 4
Safety Zone

ZONE 3
Reduce Fuel Zone

ZONE 2
Firebreak Zone

ZONE 1
Structure Ignition Zone

RIDE OUT AN INFERNO

When a fire is approaching, the smart thing to do is leave. Early. The number one cause of death in wildfires is evacuating too late. When firefighters issue an evacuation order, you should go. But let's say, for some reason, you didn't leave. You didn't get out in time, and now the road is covered in smoke, power lines are down, and the road is covered with embers. You can't just hop in the car and drive away now. So what do you do?

Terrifyingly, you stay inside. Radiant heat is the biggest concern during a raging wildfire. So simply put, the house is the safest place to be. The risk, obviously, is your house going up in flames, too. Make certain you take fire safety seriously and firescape your home before you have to. You can't clear brush from around your home when it's already burning. The second leading cause of death in wildfires? People outside the home trying to defend it from every ember. Getting into a running shower may give you some protection.

Assuming you've survived, the real time to be outside defending your home, surprisingly enough, is after the fire has passed. Many homes actually catch fire from residual embers that are burning in clogged gutters, wood piles, leaf litter, and the like. These vulnerable areas can absolutely be taken care of, sometimes with a simple bucket of water. Plan ahead, though. You will need to have a pump and water to protect your home from fire, and those might not be available in an emergency situation.

135

SURVIVE A WILDFIRE

You're out on a hike or a hunt or just a stroll, and the next thing you know, you're running for your life from a wildfire. What do you do to survive? I'm not going to lie. Surviving a wildfire is tough, but here are some tactics to try:

GET OUT A lot of people want to wait around to see how things develop. But wildfires can chew up land at 70 mph (113 km/h). By the time you realize you're in immediate danger, it's often too late.

KNOW THE AREA If you're out someplace you've never been, maintain situational awareness at all times. And have a plan of escape.

GET DOWNHILL Fire moves fastest uphill. That's bad news, because people move slowest when running uphill. Avoid draws and canyons; look for the escape that leads to open, lower elevation.

DROP YOUR GEAR Get yourself out. Trying to run with gear or staying around too long trying to pack things up will only slow you down.

GET LOW If the fire has caught up to you, look for the lowest point you can find and get into it. Think ditch, culvert, or wash out.

USE YOUR CLOTHES If you have a canteen full of water, wet your shirt and cover your face with it. Breathing through wet cloth will help you avoid smoke inhalation.

CLEAR A SPACE If you come across an open area that's already burned and free of fuel, riding out the fire there might be your best bet. Be prepared—it's going to be an oven. Radiant temperatures are deadly, even in a blackened area. Don't try burning out a space on your own. You'll likely just start the fire that kills you.

SHELTER IN PLACE And by shelter, we're talking about a fire shelter. These are small, lightweight tents that can reflect as much as 95 percent of a fire's radiant heat. Make sure you're clear of any snags or overhangs that can fall on you; pop open the shelter, and pray.

136 RECOGNIZE A FIRE WHIRL

When a fire reaches the point that it is creating its own wind, a possible outcome is a fire whirl. Mostly, fire whirls are just cool to look at, but they can be a serious issue. Temperatures in the core of a fire whirl can reach 2,000°F (1093°C), which is hot enough to reignite ash and burned debris sucked into it. The vortex can then send these burning embers in new directions, igniting structures and unburned areas.

If you really want to freak yourself out, a 2013 report verified that an EF-2 tornado in Australia was spawned from Pyrocumulonimbus clouds and the winds from a wildfire. That's right. A fire's winds were strong enough to create a supercell thunderstorm, which then spawned an EF-2 tornado inside the wildfire that created it. The fire whirl was ⅓ mile (500 m) in diameter.

The most extreme examples of fire whirls are from taken from the history books. During the 1923 Kanto Earthquake on the Japanese main island of Honshu, a firestorm erupted, spawning a massive fire whirl that killed 38,000 people in just 15 minutes. Similarly, in 1926 in San Luis Obispo, California, lightning strikes caused a four-day conflagration at an oil storage facility. Numerous whirls resulted from the fire, causing structural damage well away from the center of it. These whirls were responsible for the deaths of two people and hurled burning embers and debris as far as 3 miles (5 km) away.

137

KNOW WHEN TO FLEE

Before attempting to put out any fire, even if you do have the right extinguisher, ask yourself the following questions.

Has someone called the fire department? Do you have a clear exit route so you won't be trapped while approaching the fire? Do you have the right type of extinguisher for the type of fire? Is the extinguisher large enough for the fire? Is the fire small and contained?

If the answer to any of these questions is no, evacuate immediately. Your safety is your highest priority.

138 USE A FIRE EXTINGUISHER

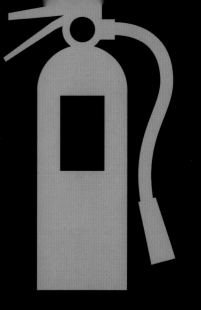

Looking for something to read on a quiet evening? Check out the instructions for your fire extinguisher. It's good to know how to use that thing before you're faced with an inferno, and you can call the rules to mind by remembering PASS: Pull, aim, squeeze, and sweep.

STEP ONE Pull the pin from the handle of the extinguisher.

STEP TWO Aim the nozzle at the base of the flames, not at the flames themselves.

STEP THREE Squeeze the handle to release short bursts of spray to knock down the flames and longer pulls to fully extinguish them.

STEP FOUR Sweep side to side until the fire is out. You typically have about ten seconds of operating time before the extinguisher is empty.

139 STOCK FIRE SAFETY GEAR

Want to protect your family, pets, and vital documents? Go beyond extinguishers and smoke alarms with these fire-safety extras.

COLLAPSIBLE FIRE-ESCAPE LADDER Home fires often fill stairwells and hallways, making the obvious escape routes unsafe. A number of manufacturers sell emergency ladders that roll and fold to a very small size for easy storage. When you need the ladder, you can quickly unfurl it, hook it over a windowsill, and climb down to safety. Ideally, you should have a ladder in every upstairs bedroom.

FIREFIGHTER ALERT SIGNS You may be overcome by smoke or otherwise unable to communicate. Or firefighters may be rushing into your home so quickly that there's no time to get their attention. That's when stickers or signs alerting rescuers to the presence of children and pets can be lifesavers. Many fire departments give out these stickers—call your local department to find out if it is one of them. Or make your own—be sure to laminate them so they're sturdy.

FIRE SAFE Stow important paper documents and backups of electronic files in a fireproof, waterproof safe in your home, along with any irreplaceable sentimental items. These safes range in size from tiny to enormous, to accommodate your particular needs.

140

INSTALL SMOKE DETECTORS

Trust me: If a fire ever starts in your home, you'll want to know about it. So make sure there's at least one smoke alarm in every room of your house, except for bathrooms and closets.

SAVE THE DATE Before mounting your smoke detector, write the date of purchase on the alarm. (After eight years pass, swap it out for a new one.)

HANG IT HIGH You know the old adage about smoke rising? It's true. So mount your detector on the ceiling away from windows and doors and at least 4 inches (10 cm) from the wall. Avoid placing one in the path of heat or steam coming from the kitchen or bathroom; otherwise it'll go off all the time.

MOUNT IT RIGHT All smoke detectors come with specific mounting instructions. Most make it easy for you: Installation requires little more than a screwdriver and two screws. Some types are even adhesive.

TEST IT OFTEN You should check your detector once a month to ensure that it's working properly. Simply push the button until you hear a loud noise confirming that all's as it should be. If there's no sound, you've got a dud—replace it.

KEEP BATTERIES FRESH Replace the battery once a year. If it starts making an annoying chirping sound, that's your cue that it's time for new juice.

141 DON'T TRUST THE COLD

Imagine that it's the end of September and you're enjoying a warm fall day at your home in Minnesota. A dry cold front passed through the area a few hours ago, bringing a couple of clouds but none of the rain that typically comes with storm systems that swing through the area. Even though the feature was a cold front, it acted more like a dry line you'd see in Oklahoma—dew points dropped significantly, but temperatures didn't budge too much.

The combination of gusty winds behind the front, warm temperatures, and low relative humidity levels all primed the environment for brushfires. By nightfall, hundreds of acres of countryside burn as a result of homeowners burning leaves, running gas-powered equipment in brush, or flicking cigarettes out the car window, despite a red flag warning that implores citizens to refrain from these careless activities.

This scenario isn't that far-fetched—situations like this occur frequently in locations where warmer temperatures, low humidity, and breezy conditions come together just right to allow fires to form. It doesn't feel like you're sitting in a tinderbox in western Colorado, but the silent danger exists just the same.

142 BE YOUR OWN CHIMNAEY SWEEP

Heating fires are responsible for more than a third of all U.S. house fires, and most of them occur due to creosote buildup in the chimney. This mixture of incompletely burned flammable substances, soot, and condensed gases forms an oily coating inside your chimney that can burst into flames.

You can reduce buildup by using only seasoned hardwoods (other flammables leave more deposits) and keeping your fireplace or woodstove clean. However, creosote will accumulate regardless, so you should clean out your chimney at least once a year. You'll also be able to clear out anything else stuck in there that could be a fire hazard.

Set up a tarp around your fireplace to keep the inside of your house tidy when cleaning your chimney, and sweep or vacuum up any ash, soot, creosote, or other contaminants. The chimney itself can then be swept out with a long scrubbing brush, usually one with a spiraling head. You also can make do by lining a burlap sack with chicken wire, filling it with rocks or small weights, and lowering it down the chimney on a rope to scrape the sides. Various chimney-cleaning solvents are available, or you can use kerosene to help break up the stuff.

143

HOLD YOUR BREATH

Wildfires, a house fire, or even a bonfire can expose you to harmful levels of smoke. Hot smoke can be the most dangerous, as it can burn your throat or lungs, and contain harmful gases.

Signs of smoke inhalation can include the following: coughing; difficulty breathing; hoarse voice or difficulty speaking; nausea or vomiting; headache; or feeling sleepy, disoriented, or confused. If you notice someone with any combination of these symptoms, get them out into fresh air and call emergency responders for help.

144 STOP, DROP, AND ROLL

What do you do if your clothing catches on fire and there's no fire extinguisher or water source nearby? Your answer is simple and effective: Stop, drop, and roll. Be sure that any kids in your household know this technique, and review it annually as part of any fire drills you conduct for the family. If you see someone else on fire, yell "Stop, drop, and roll!" at them. They will likely be panicked, so you may need to repeat it a couple of times. You also can help smother the fire but be sure to smother towards his or her feet so as to not push the flames up to his or her face.

STOP Be sure you're away from the source of the fire and on a surface you can roll around on. Any unneeded movement will fan the flames and thus increase your chances of being burned by them.

DROP Lay down on the ground while covering your eyes, nose, and mouth with your hands.

ROLL Roll over and back and forth until the flames are out. Remove any burned clothing immediately.

145 ESCAPE A BURNING HOUSE

The key to surviving a fire in your home is having an effective plan in place before the smoldering starts.

KNOW WHERE TO GO Visibility is nearly zero in smoky conditions, so you need to know your escape route by heart. For rooms that have more than one exit, consider which of them would work best in different situations. Practice evacuating with a blindfold on, with someone watching you to keep you safe.

STAY LOW Heat rises; so do smoke and flames. If you're exiting a burning building, get on your hands and knees and crawl toward the nearest safe exit. Cover your mouth and nose with a damp cloth to fight smoke inhalation.

ANTICIPATE Before you open a door, feel for heat on the flat surface rather than the doorknob, which could be dangerously hot. Look under the door, too, for visible flames. If there's any doubt, head to a secondary exit.

SHUN STAIRS If you're trapped on an upper level, get out through a window (have escape ladders at the ready for just such an emergency). Don't use a stairway, because it can act like a chimney, funneling heat and smoke upward.

DON'T BE A HERO Under no circumstance should you remain inside to fight a blaze. If an initial flare-up is not immediately contained, evacuate right away. Run outside, call 911, and let the fire department put out the flames.

146

PREPARE FOR THE END OF THE WORLD AS WE KNOW IT

It's quite clear that weather can kill any of us. And that it can, in catastrophic cases, kill hundreds, even thousands, of people. But can bad weather kill everybody? Depending on what caused that weather, the answer is probably yes.

Some cataclysmic event like a meteor or comet striking the Earth would have dramatic consequences on global weather, and it's hard to think of a scenario in which most people who lived through the disaster would survive very long. The dinosaurs were much tougher and angrier than we are, and look at how well they fared when the comet struck.

Let's say a rather large meteor careens through the atmosphere and strikes the ocean. Assuming that you survive the ensuing tsunamis, earthquakes, and initial rain of debris, the future still looks pretty bleak. Hurricane activity would cease due to a lack of heat necessary to warm ocean waters, which doesn't sound so bad—except for the fact that nothing else would be warm either. Fine particles would remain suspended in the atmosphere for months and years after impact, obscuring the sun to the point that plant life would die out within months. The lack of sunlight would also steadily plunge temperatures, leading to cold days and frigid nights around the world. Once plants and animals die off, even resourceful humans would run out of food.

In other words, the change in weather after a meteor impact would ensure that not only humans but most life on Earth would come to a swift, grim demise. Sleep tight!

147 STUDY SOLAR FLARES

A solar flare occurs when magnetic energy builds up in the sun's atmosphere and then is suddenly released, thus emitting radiation across much of the electromagnetic spectrum. The amount of energy released in a solar flare can be massive—the equivalent of millions of thermonuclear bombs exploding simultaneously.

Flares are rated in various classes according to their intensity, similar to the Richter scale for earthquakes, in that each category is 10 times stronger than the one before it. A-, B-, and C-class flares have no significant impacts, but M-class eruptions can generate brief radio blackouts at the poles and cause minor radiation increases that can endanger orbiting astronauts. X-class flares, however, can potentially affect systems on a planet-wide scale, triggering a number of impacts on technology-dependent systems.

148 SPACE OUT

Your general disaster-planning efforts will also apply to space weather, but, obviously, there is really nothing preventative possible, given the cosmic nature of the threat. Being aware of the impacts and making plans to cope with them are the best ways to handle this particular type of disaster.

The three types of effects you are likely to deal with are blackouts, electronics failures, and GPS or communications disruptions. To cope with a lack of navigation, paper maps in your car disaster kit will aid your ability to navigate not only during a solar flare but anytime your GPS isn't able to acquire a signal. Since communications will also likely be affected, having predesignated meeting places for members of your household allows you to convene even when you can't directly communicate.

149 BE AWARE OF X-CLASS FLARES

The strongest class of solar flares can have a serious effect on technological-dependent systems, several of which can impact millions of people regionally or on large parts of the globe.

An X-class solar flare can disrupt GPS signals, thus hindering not only navigation critical to aviation, shipping, and personal use but also global financial systems dependent on GPS signals to time-stamp transactions. Likewise, the flare can interrupt satellite-based TV, radio, Internet, and voice communications, such as satellite phones.

Electrical power grids can also suffer disruption from an X-class flare. While measures have been taken to prevent widespread problems, the distribution system may still be vulnerable.

Other impacts can include spacecraft anomalies, disruptions in telephone, transportation, and fuel distribution systems; pipelines and drilling; and air- and ship-based magnetic surveys.

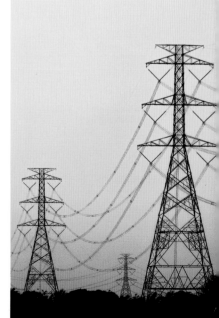

FIND WHAT YOU'RE LOOKING FOR.

You may have had less than enjoyable experiences in the past with really dry and uninspiring material about safety, disasters, and preparedness. You may have noticed that this book is colorfully designed to be easy to read, with subjects broken down in bite-size pieces that won't overwhelm you with information and detail you don't need. It provides an introduction to a wide variety of skills and strategies that will be helpful in a wide range of circumstances. Use it as a broad reference guide or pick and choose just the content that feels most relevant to your needs. This index of specific tips and subject matter will help you find exactly what you need—when you need it.

INDEX

INDEX

CREDITS

Waterbury Publications, Inc., Des Moines, IA

Creative Director Ken Carlson
Editorial Director Lisa Kingsley
Associate Design Director Doug Samuelson
Associate Editor Tricia Bergman
Production Designer Mindy Samuelson
Copy Editor Jo First
Proofreader Linda Wagner

PHOTOGRAPHY CREDITS All images courtesy of Shutterstock unless otherwise noted: iStock: pg. 4, 14 Winter Myths: Canadapanda / Shutterstock.com, Extreme Weather Around the World: Bangladesh: AP Photo/Pavel Rahman, Get the Truth: Alexey Stiop / Shutterstock.com: 73 Wikimedia Commons: pg. 7, 136

ILLUSTRATION CREDITS Conor Buckley: 13, 30, 31, 34, 47, 64, 65, 93, 103, 104, 106, 117, 127 Hayden Foell: 22, 28, 51, 68 Liberum Donum: 1, 50, 66, 69, 94, 95, 133, 144 Christine Meighan: 23, 32, 78, 86 Lauren Towner: 132

ABOUT THE MAGAZINE

Since it was founded in 1898, *Outdoor Life* magazine has provided survival tips, wilderness skills, gear reports, and other essential information for hands-on outdoor enthusiasts. Each issue delivers the best advice in sportsmanship as well as thrilling true-life tales, detailed gear reviews, insider hunting, shooting, and fishing hints, and much more to nearly 1 million readers. Its survival-themed Web site also covers disaster preparedness and the skills you need to thrive anywhere from the backcountry to the urban jungles.

OUTDOOR LIFE

Chief Executive Officer
Eric Zinczenko

Vice President, Publishing Director
Gregory D. Gatto

Editorial Director Anthony Licata

Editor-in-Chief Andrew McKean

Managing Editor Jean McKenna

Senior Deputy Editor John B. Snow

Deputy Editor Gerry Bethge

Assistant Managing Editor
Margaret M. Nussey

Assistant Editor Natalie Krebs

Senior Administrative Assistant
Maribel Martin

Design Director Sean Johnston

Art Director Brian Struble

Associate Art Directors
Russ Smith, James A. Walsh

Photography Director John Toolan

Photo Editor Justin Appenzeller

Production Manager Judith Weber

Digital Director Nate Matthews

Online Content Editor Alex Robinson

weldonowen

President & Publisher Roger Shaw

Associate Publisher Mariah Bear

SVP, Sales & Marketing
Amy Kaneko

Finance Director Philip Paulick

Editor Ian Cannon

Creative Director Kelly Booth

Art Director Allister Fein

Illustration Coordinator
Conor Buckley

Production Director Chris Hemesath

Production Manager
Michelle Duggan

Director of Enterprise Systems
Shawn Macey

Imaging Manager Don Hill

Weldon Owen would like to thank Molly Stewart for editorial assistance, and Kevin Broccoli for the index.

© 2016 Weldon Owen Inc.
1045 Sansome Street, suite 100
San Francisco, CA 94111
www.weldonowen.com

BONNIER

ISBN 978-168188-102-7
10 9 8 7 6 5 4 3 2 1
2016 2017 2018 2019
Printed in China by RR Donnelley

NIGHTWING
VOL.4 BLOCKBUSTER

NIGHTWING

VOL.4 BLOCKBUSTER

TIM SEELEY
writer

JAVIER FERNANDEZ * **MIGUEL MENDONÇA**
MINKYU JUNG * **VICENTE CIFUENTES** * **DIANA EGEA**
artists

CHRIS SOTOMAYOR
colorist

CARLOS M. MANGUAL
letterer

MARCUS TO and CHRIS SOTOMAYOR
collection cover artists

NIGHTWING created by **MARV WOLFMAN** and **GEORGE PÉREZ**
HUNTRESS created by **PAUL LEVITZ, BOB LAYTON** and **JOE STATON**
SPYRAL created by **GRANT MORRISON, CHRIS BURNHAM** and **YANICK PAQUETTE**

REBECCA TAYLOR Editor - Original Series ✳ **DAVE WIELGOSZ** Assistant Editor - Original Series
JEB WOODARD Group Editor - Collected Editions ✳ **ERIKA ROTHBERG** Editor - Collected Edition
STEVE COOK Design Director - Books ✳ **MONIQUE NARBONETA** Publication Design

BOB HARRAS Senior VP - Editor-in-Chief, DC Comics
PAT McCALLUM Executive Editor, DC Comics

DIANE NELSON President ✳ **DAN DiDIO** Publisher ✳ **JIM LEE** Publisher ✳ **GEOFF JOHNS** President & Chief Creative Officer
AMIT DESAI Executive VP - Business & Marketing Strategy, Direct to Consumer & Global Franchise Management
SAM ADES Senior VP & General Manager, Digital Services ✳ **BOBBIE CHASE** VP & Executive Editor, Young Reader & Talent Development
MARK CHIARELLO Senior VP - Art, Design & Collected Editions ✳ **JOHN CUNNINGHAM** Senior VP - Sales & Trade Marketing
ANNE DePIES Senior VP - Business Strategy, Finance & Administration ✳ **DON FALLETTI** VP - Manufacturing Operations
LAWRENCE GANEM VP - Editorial Administration & Talent Relations ✳ **ALISON GILL** Senior VP - Manufacturing & Operations
HANK KANALZ Senior VP - Editorial Strategy & Administration ✳ **JAY KOGAN** VP - Legal Affairs ✳ **JACK MAHAN** VP - Business Affairs
NICK J. NAPOLITANO VP - Manufacturing Administration ✳ **EDDIE SCANNELL** VP - Consumer Marketing
COURTNEY SIMMONS Senior VP - Publicity & Communications ✳ **JIM (SKI) SOKOLOWSKI** VP - Comic Book Specialty Sales & Trade Marketing
NANCY SPEARS VP - Mass, Book, Digital Sales & Trade Marketing ✳ **MICHELE R. WELLS** VP - Content Strategy

NIGHTWING VOLUME 4: BLOCKBUSTER

DC Comics, 2900 West Alameda Ave., Burbank, CA 91505
Printed by LSC Communications, Kendallville, IN, USA. 12/15/17. First Printing.
ISBN: 978-1-4012-7533-4

Library of Congress Cataloging-in-Publication Data is available.

PEFC Certified

Printed on paper from
sustainably managed
forests, controlled
sources

PEFC/29-31-337   www.pefc.org

circus into a city. And this ol' **trapeze artist** is right at home.

After a quiet month where the only action I saw involved a time-freezing dude-bro, things suddenly got really...**loud.**

On one side, the **Simon Project Kings,** a crew out of **Metropolis** shooting their way through enemy territory.

On the other, the **Tail's End Noughts,** a local gang claiming said "**territory.**"

TIM SEELEY **WRITER**

MIGUEL MENDONÇA **PENCILS**

VICENTE CIFUENTES **INKS**

CHRIS SOTOMAYOR **COLORS**

CARLOS M. MANGUAL **LETTERS**

PAUL RENAUD **COVER**

DAVE WIELGOSZ **ASST. EDITOR**

REBECCA TAYLOR **EDITOR**

BLOCKBUSTER PART ONE

KRAKOOM

Heavy-duty knock-off alien weapons. Supplied by a mysterious seller called *the Second Hand*.

But why would the Kings start a fight? What do the Noughts have that they want?

Why not take their gear and go be Superman's problem?

YOU-- YOU SAVED MY LIFE, MAN.

YEAH, WELL, DON'T GET TOO EXCITED.

I ALSO BROUGHT *THE COPS*.

WHEEOOOWHEE

PO-PO WASN'T PART OF *THE DEAL*.

DROP THE WEAPONS! DOWN!

WE OUT LIKE *STAR TREK*!

VZZZ

The month's worth of quiet wasn't because the criminals had hung up the sign and closed shop.

It was anticipation...

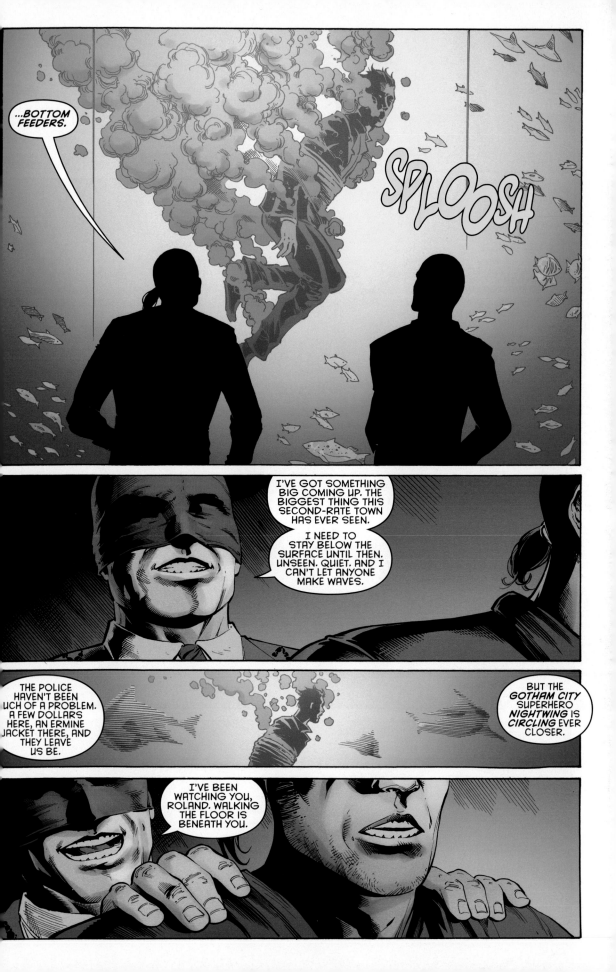

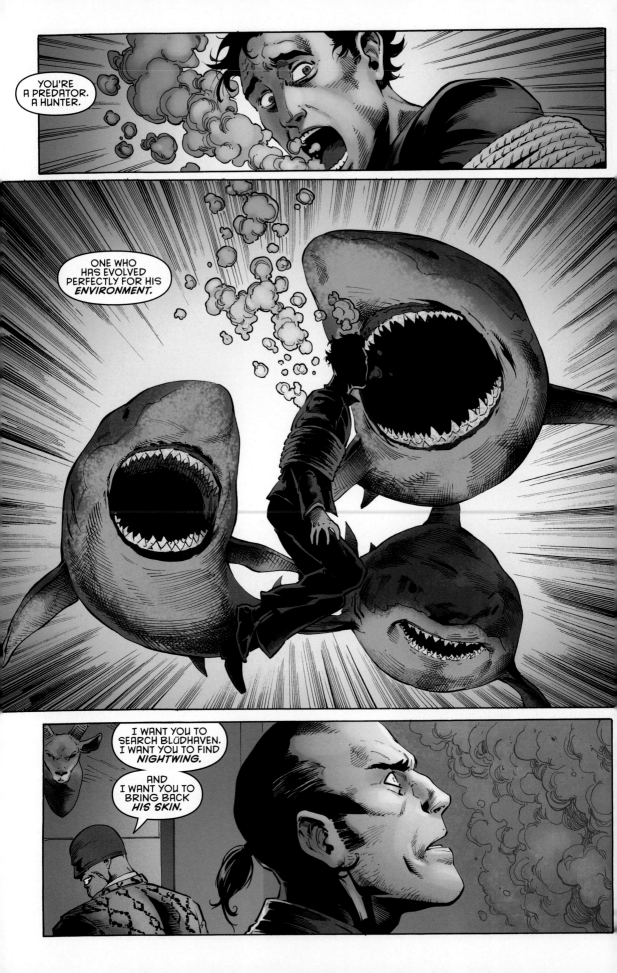

THE THING IS, I KNOW SHE'S RIGHT. I CAN'T *VOLUNTEER* FOREVER.

BUT I HAVE A PRETTY SHORT ATTENTION SPAN FOR JOBS. I'VE NEVER KEPT ONE FOR VERY LONG.

AND, I GUESS I NEVER CONSIDERED WHAT I WANTED TO DO FOR A CAREER BECAUSE I WAS ENJOYING THE... *VOLUNTEER WORK* SO MUCH.

PLUS, MY FIRST REAL JOB WAS IN A *CIRCUS*. SURE, THERE WERE NO BENEFITS AND MY CO-WORKERS WERE MONKEYS, BUT IT'S STILL PRETTY TOUGH TO BEAT.

ANYWAY, SORRY I'M DROPPING ALL OF THIS ON YOU GUYS.

S'ALRIGHT, MR. GRAYSON.

YOU'VE BEEN LISTENING TO ME, *GIZ* AND THE OTHER *RUN-OFFS*--Err, I MEAN "*THE EX-OFFENDERS' SUPPORT GROUP*" FOR THE PAST FEW MONTHS.

ONLY FAIR WE RETURNED THE FAVOR.

CHIT!

I don't hang out at the Saddle just for the **stool-cushion** therapy.

The happy cowboy's backside also happens to be a great place to hide an extra Nightwing costume.

Giz wasn't wrong. And I do want Shawn to be happy.

But people who hire Stallion's kind of muscle are coming into town tomorrow at the Tail's End docks...just a few blocks from Tail's High.

That's why the Kings attacked. They got a deal on their gear from someone who wanted that neighborhood to themselves. Someone who's bringing **death rays** into Blüdhaven.

Someone **big**.

NIGHTWING.

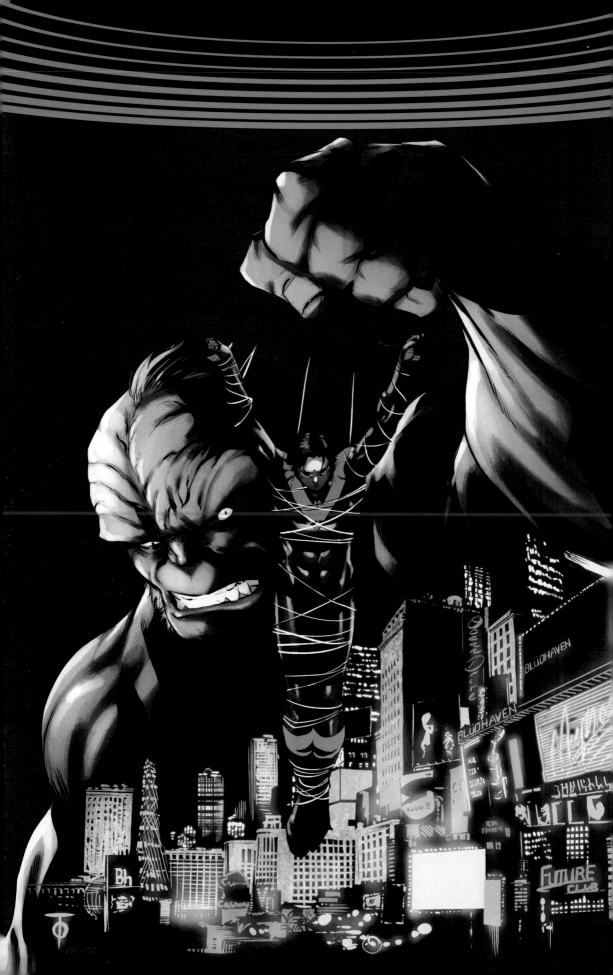

"MARK DESMOND WAS THE ORIGINAL *BLOCKBUSTER.*

"SEE, MARK WAS A CHEMIST. A PRETTY DAMN GOOD ONE. BUT HE ALWAYS LACKED IN THE *PHYSICALITY* DEPARTMENT.

"SO HE MADE A GLOWING GREEN CONCOCTION THAT INCREASED HIS STRENGTH.

"PROBLEM WAS, IT ALSO MADE HIM EXTREMELY AGGRESSIVE AND DUMBER THAN A BAG OF HAMMERS.

"EVEN WORSE, IT MADE HIM EASY TO *MANIPULATE...*"

TIM SEELEY WRITER
MINKYU JUNG ARTIST
CHRIS SOTOMAYOR COLORIST
CARLOS M. MANGUAL LETTERER
MARCUS TO & CHRIS SOTOMAYOR COVER ARTISTS
DAVE WIELGOSZ ASST. EDITOR
REBECCA TAYLOR EDITOR

BLOCKBUSTER PART TWO

Ahem I said... thwarting killer robots.

INCOMING PROJECTILE.

I'm not sure any of that has prepared me to be a dockworker.

WOK

HNF!

Maybe I need to goose the old résumé a little. Learn a new skill.

I know...

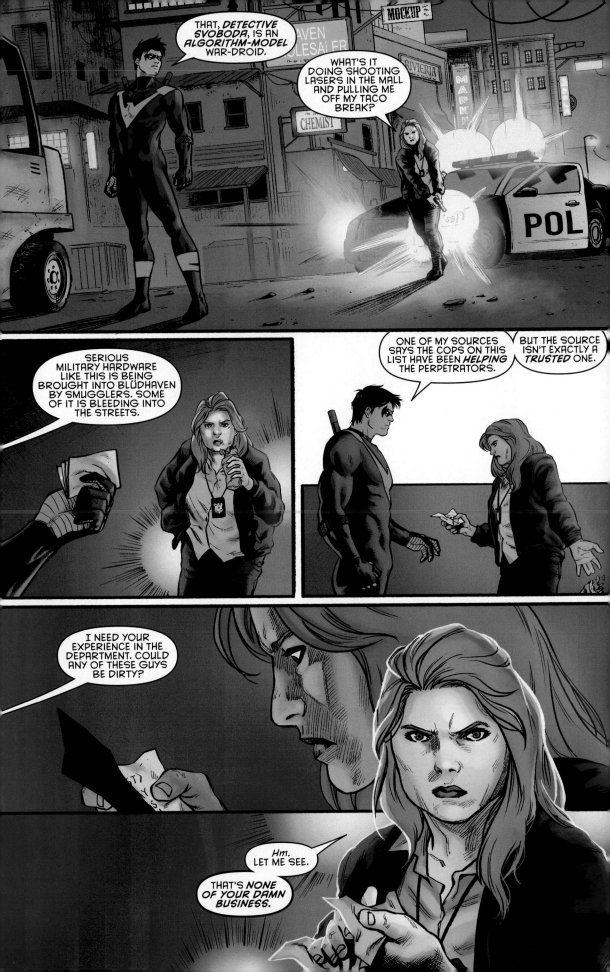

TAIL'S END BAY.

First I had an argument with Detective Svoboda. And then that uncomfortable conversation with Shawn.

It says something that the best talk I've had recently was with a guy who turns into a monster.

But if Roland Desmond is right, *Charlie Dulcover* and *Griffin Bratt* are drawing more than just a BPD paycheck.

If they're picking up shipments in the bay, they'd need a location that's quiet and out of sight.

Like that for instance. *Ambergris Island,* a massive partly sunken whaling ship that the city never got around to cleaning up.

Except this looks less like a pickup and more like a drop-off. Evidence-locker crates.

THINK THE GUESTS WILL MIND IF I SAMPLE ONE OF THE PARTY FAVORS?

Party favors? Who goes to a party in a rusting iron death trap?

WELCOME, FRIENDS!

ON DISPLAY YOU'LL FIND AN ARRAY OF WEAPONS THAT *TIGER SHARK* PROMISES WILL HELP YOU RID YOURSELF OF YOUR CITY'S *SUPERHERO* PROBLEM.

OH, NO REASON.

Okay. Actually, reasons.

One: I was given the names of police officers who might have had a hand in bringing illegal high-tech weapons to Blüdhaven.

Two: The source of those names, *Roland Desmond,* actually sold me out to the pirate *Tiger Shark.*

Three: Tiger Shark intended for me to be used as a guinea pig for the super-crooks testing out his weapons.

TIM SEELEY WRITER
MIGUEL MENDONCA PENCILS
DIANA EGEA INKS
CHRIS SOTOMAYOR COLORS
CARLOS M. MANGUAL LETTERS
PAUL RENAUD COVER
DAVE WIELGOSZ ASST. EDITOR
REBECCA TAYLOR EDITOR

BLOCKBUSTER
PART THREE

HOW'S *YOUR* LOVE LIFE, *MOUSE?*

PRETTY MUCH NONEXISTENT. BRENDAN TOOK ANOTHER *FREELANCE* GIG. WON'T SAY WHAT IT IS.

IF HE'S STRIPPING, HE BETTER LET THOSE GIRLS KNOW HIS SKINNY LI'L BUTT IS ALL MINE.

HEH. AT LEAST HE'S WORKING. I COULDN'T EVEN GET *DICK* TO GO TO AN INTERVIEW--

WHAT?!

NO FUNDS

PAM, LOOK AT THIS CRAP! "NO AVAILABLE FUNDS." THE CITY IS CUTTING OUR BUDGET AGAIN!

IT'S OKAY, SHAWN. WE'LL FIGURE IT OUT--

NO, WE WON'T! THE POLITICIANS AND BUREAUCRATS HAVE BEEN *DRAINING* US DRY, ONE DROP AT A TIME ALREADY!

HOW AM I SUPPOSED TO RUN A CENTER ON *THIS?* HOW AM I SUPPOSED TO DO ANY GOOD?

MAYBE SAVE THIS FOR THE *RUN-OFFS* GROUP--

UH. SHAWN?

Crash. Assassin and crime boss who borrowed some jet-boots from Steel.

Avery Martell, leader of the Whale's Enders gang.

THERE, SKYHOOK!

The demonic, winged liver paté from earlier and a Eastern European royal that can make me queasy.

AH! AHHH!

Instincts tell me: not here, not yet, and move that ass.

GIZ TO BLUE CHEESE!

YOU CAN CALL ME NIGHTWING, GIZ. IT'S ALREADY A CODE NAME.

RIGHT! I GOT A BLUEPRINT! GOOD NEWS!

THERE'S A PERSONAL ESCAPE CAPSULE ON DECK THREE.

YOUR DEATH WILL ARM VLATAVA!

URG. I--I FEEL... UNWELL.

Always take advantage of your surroundings.

And the bad guys' inability to focus on anyone but themselves.

BLARGHF!

YOU FOUL, FILTHY BEAST!

GIZ! I'M AT THE MEZZANINE. WHERE NEXT?

THE POD ACCESS IS THROUGH THE SECURITY DOOR.

COMPARED TO WHAT I'VE GONE THROUGH TO GET HERE, THAT SHOULDN'T BE A PROBLEM.

ALL YOU'VE GOTTA DO IS GET THROUGH THIS ROOM.

Clock King. Former engineer who builds clockwork death traps.

Shado. Mistress of the Japanese bow martial art, Kyudo.

Sleek. Elegant. Controlled. Distant.

Sooner or later, she'll hit her mark from a nice cozy position.

Clock King. Former engineer who builds clockwork deathtraps.

Just one of the many super-villains *Tiger Shark* sicced on me after Blockbuster conned me into coming to his "party."

Clocky here has the "*time vest*," from a cache of high-tech alien weapons Tiger Shark has been selling in Blüdhaven.

ESCAPE P

It freezes time in a bubble around the user.

I'm going to invade his personal space.

04

TIM SEELEY WRITER
MINKYU JUNG ARTIST
CHRIS SOTOMAYOR COLORS
CARLOS M. MANGUAL LETTERS
BRAD WALKER, ANDREW HENNESSY & CHRIS SOTOMAYOR COVER
DAVE WIELGOSZ ASST. EDITOR
REBECCA TAYLOR EDITOR

BLOCKBUSTER
FINALE

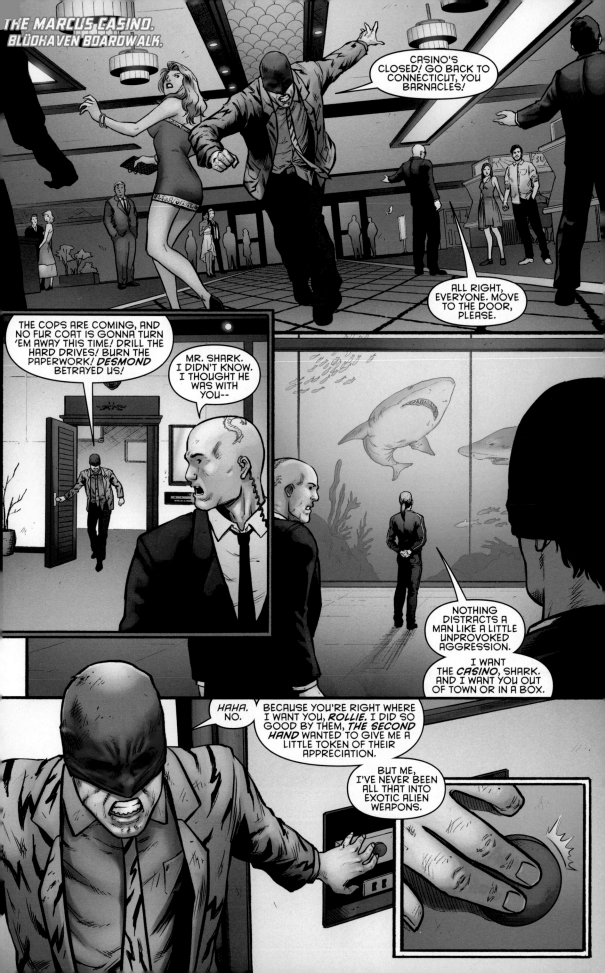

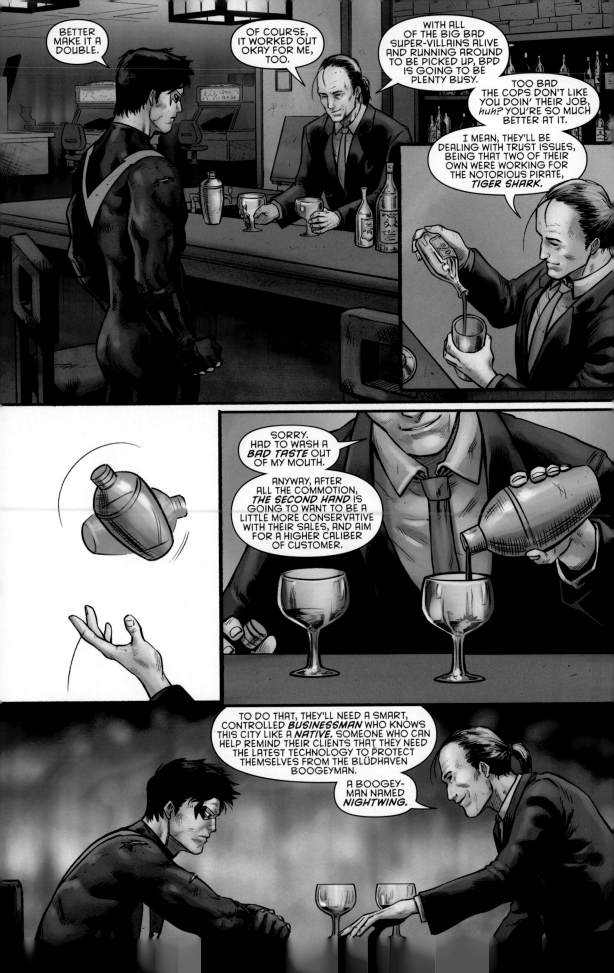

When I put on the "time vest," I slipped between moments, living one second over and over.

I wish that second could be this one.

The moment right after I land on the ledge. After I open up the window.

When I first see Shawn after being away. When I hold her tight and tell her...

...I love you.

She doesn't hug back. Her usually warm, soft embrace replaced by cold, rigid silence.

SHAWN. PLEASE. I--

I'M SORRY, DICK.

WHY?

NEXT: **THIS IS A JOB FOR HUNTRESS...
AND AGENT 37**

When someone dies, their passing does something strange to everyone who knew them.

It forces a reset.

In the seconds, minutes, days after, you ask what life will be like without the departed.

You ask if there are things you should have said. Should have done.

And whether you could have stopped it.

Brendan "Giz" Li was a programmer, a hacker, a former super-villain and a friend.

He was killed while researching illegal high-tech weapons smuggled into the Blüd by an organization called *the Second Hand.*

HE WAS GOOD, STALLION. HE NEVER RELAPSED INTO CRIME. HE WAS THE BEST OF US.

HEY, IF IT MAKES YA FEEL BETTER, DEVIL, HE WEREN'T *THAT* GOOD. HE NEVER DID PAY HIS BAR TAB.

I asked Giz to look into the weapons. Told him not to go too far. I thought he'd be safe.

He dug and dug and it got him murdered.

No one wants to say it, but they blame Nightwing, at least a little. No one except for maybe my ex-girlfriend, *Shawn Tsang.*

The address Argento provided leads us to a luxury summer house in the hills overlooking the city.

I can't help but get even angrier. This scumbag who visited such ugliness on a good man gets to live among all this beauty.

And maybe that's it. I lied to Shawn, to myself. I *can* be just as motivated by *rage* as anyone else.

I just choose to be around people who might act on it...

...so I don't have to.

DRACUL.

NOT AS *IMMORTAL* AS HIS NAMESAKE, APPARENTLY.

DOUBLE TAPPED IN THE BACK OF THE HEAD. MOB STYLE.

GIANNI GOT WHACKED BY ONE OF HIS OWN. ARGENTO? ONE OF HIS FREELANCERS?

ON THE DESK. A KNIFE, A GUN AND A *PHOTO* OF THE MADONNA.

THESE THREE 'TEMS TOGETHER ARE USED IN MAFIA INITIATION.

THE INITIATE KISSES EACH ITEM. THEN, THE KNIFE IS USED TO CUT HIS HAND. THE INITIATE DROPS BLOOD UPON THE MADONNA AND SAYS *"MAY MY BODY BE DESTROYED LIKE THIS CARD IF I EVER BETRAY CASA NOSTRA."*

THEN THE PHOTO IS LIT BY CANDLE FLAME. IT IS AN IMPORTANT PART OF THE RITE.

THIS *SHOULD NOT* BE HERE.

SKRSH

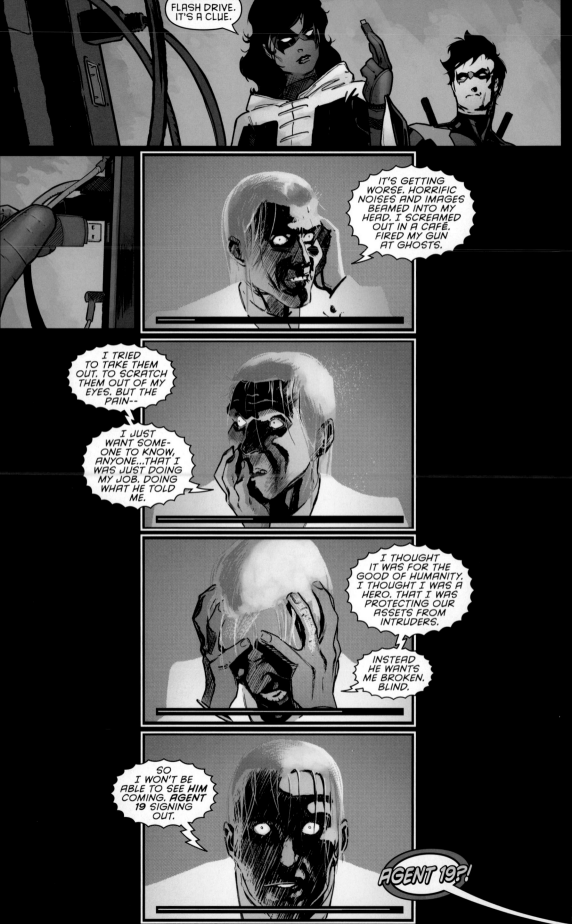

Name's Grayson. **Dick.** Former spy. Current superhero.

As Nightwing, I've spent the past few months hunting down high-tech arms dealers called **the Second Hand** on the streets of **Blüdhaven.**

The strain consumed my life. I pushed my girlfriend, **Shawn,** away. All the way.

Then the Hand retaliated against my efforts by murdering my friend, Brendan "Giz" Li, after he hacked into one of their weapons.

NIGHTWING AND THE HUNTRESS IN...

With **the Huntress'** help, I tracked his assassin here to Palermo...

...only to discover that Spyral and the Second Hand are **one and the same.**

I believe the technical term for this situation is a "sucks donut."

TIGER KING OF KANDAHAR. CODE NAME: AGENT ONE.

WHAT THE HELL, TIG?! WE'RE OLD PARTNERS! SPYRAL WENT LEGIT!

As in, "When your friends go bad, it sucks, don't it?"

SPYRAL PART TWO

TIM SEELEY WRITER JAVIER FERNANDEZ ARTIST
CHRIS SOTOMAYOR COLORIST CARLOS M. MANGUAL LETTERER
JAVIER FERNANDEZ & CHRIS SOTOMAYOR COVER
DAVE WIELGOSZ ASST. EDITOR REBECCA TAYLOR EDITOR MARK DOYLE GROUP EDITOR

TIGER... IS HE--

ALIVE.

WE HAVEN'T GOTTEN TO *MURDER CLASS* YET AT ST. HADRIAN'S.

HOW DID YOU KNOW--?

THE RUMORS SPREAD LIKE WILD-FIRE THAT OUR *GYM TEACHER* HAD BEEN AN UNDERCOVER SUPERHERO.

AND THAT BAHOOKIE CERTAINLY DID NOT BELONG TO *SUPERMAN.*

LEAVE THE BOY BE, *MS. NUSSBAUM.* I HAVE A MORE URGENT QUESTION.

WHAT HAPPENED TO *SPYRAL?*

AND WHERE IS THE FOURTH MEMBER OF YOUR TROUPE? *MS. DUFF?*

AFTER THE BATTLE AGAINST *THE PARLIAMENT OF OWLS** OUR CURRICULUM WAS CHANGED.

"WE WERE TOLD WE WOULD INITIALLY BE FOCUSED ON 'FREELANCE PEACEKEEPING.'"

*SEE NIGHTWING: BETTER THAN BATMAN. --TAY

...TO BE MR. MINOS, THE MAN WITH THE LABYRINTH FACE.

NOW, LET'S SEE WHO'S KNOCKING AT MY DOOR.

SPYRAL FINALE

TIM SEELEY WRITER

JAVIER FERNANDEZ & MIGUEL MENDONCA PENCILS

JAVIER FERNANDEZ & DIANA EGEA INKS

CHRIS SOTOMAYOR COLORIST

CARLOS M. MANGUAL LETTERER

JAVIER FERNANDEZ & CHRIS SOTOMAYOR COVER

DAVE WIELGOSZ ASST. EDITOR

REBECCA TAYLOR EDITOR

MARK DOYLE GROUP EDITOR

...BECAUSE LIGHT CONSTRUCTS DON'T HAVE *HONKIN'* BODY ODOR.

LOTTI DUFF.

OTTI! WE CAME TO RESCUE YOU.

YEH, AND I WISH YOU WOULDN'T 'AVE. IT'S NOT SAFE. I SHUT OFF ME TRACKER, WHICH MEANS MINOS DID THE BEEPIN'.

YOU'RE HURT.

EHM. AFTER I GOT YOU LOT OUT OF THE SCHOOL, MINOS TAGGED ME AND GOT ME *PDB DEVICE*. IT DISRUPTED *SPYRALTECH* RIGHT NICELY, UNTIL HE SMASHED IT ALL UP.

IT WAS ALL I COULD DO TO SCRAMBLE THE ELITE AGENTS' BRAINS FOR A BIT AND GET TO THIS BUGHOLE.

THERE WILL BE TIME FOR SHOW-AND-TELL LATER, MS. DUFF. WE NEED TO KNOW TWO THINGS RIGHT NOW.

HOW IS MINOS ALIVE AND WHAT DOES HE WANT?

HOW'S HE ALIVE...THAS A WEE BIT COMPLICATED.

WHAT HE WANTS ISN'T.

HE WANTS *NIGHTWING*.

AND HE USED YOU ALL TO DELIVER HIM RIGHT TO HIS DOOR.

WE ARE *WOMEN OF ST. HADRIAN'S.* ANY MAN WHO USES US...WILL FACE REPERCUSSIONS.

NEVER WAS ONE TO TRUST AUTHORITY. SO I BUILT IN A BACK DOOR TO ALL THE SPYRAL TECH. WITH THE TOUCH OF A BUTTON ON MY NEW *PURE DAMN BRILLIANT 2.0* DEVICE, THAT'S THE END OF EVERY SECOND HAND WEAPON WITHIN THIRTY KILOMETERS.

THAT'LL BE A NICE PRESENT FOR *ROLAND DESMOND*.

THE SAME AI THAT CONTROLLED OUR MINDS, AND TURNED US AGAINST YOU. WE ARE SORRY.

WE OWE IT TO YOU TO FIND THESE WEAPONS WHEREVER ELSE THEY HAVE PROPAGATED.

ACTUALLY, I'M GONNA RENAME THE PDB *THE GIZMO*, AFTER YOUR FRIEND. HE GAVE HIS LIFE TO ALERT ME ABOUT THE *MINOS AI* HIDIN' IN OUR ATTIC.

GOOD-BYE, GIRLS. IT SEEMS YOU HAVE A NEW MISSION.

YOU SHOULD COME WITH US! YOU WERE OUR FAVORITE TEACHER, MATRON BERTINELLI.

AND YOU SEEMED SO AT HOME AMONG ALL THE CRAZINESS.

NO. I'M SORRY, GIRLS. SPYRAL IS NOT WHO I AM ANYMORE.

AGENT ONE DIDN'T COME TO SEE US OFF?

HE DOESN'T LIKE TO SAY GOOD-BYE. HE GETS SO CHOKED UP HE CAN'T CALL ME NAMES.

THIRTEEN HOURS LATER.

OKAY, SHAWN. DON'T SCREW THIS UP OR LET YOUR ATTITUDE GET IN THE WAY. MAYBE RUN IT THROUGH?

"DICK...I'M SORRY. I WAS COOL WHEN THINGS WERE OKAY, BUT I WAS RUNNING.

"BUT HOW WE DEAL WITH TRAGEDY...THE HARD STUFF...*THAT'S* LIFE. I WANT TO FACE THAT WITH YOU.

"YOU HANDLE ANGER BETTER THAN ANYONE ELSE. THAT USED TO PISS ME OFF.

"BUT NOW, INSTEAD OF ASKING YOU TO BE SOMETHING OTHER THAN NIGHTWING...

"I WANT US TO BE *PARTNERS* IN EVERYTHING. I WANT US TO BE--"

When someone dies, their passing does something strange to everyone who knew them.

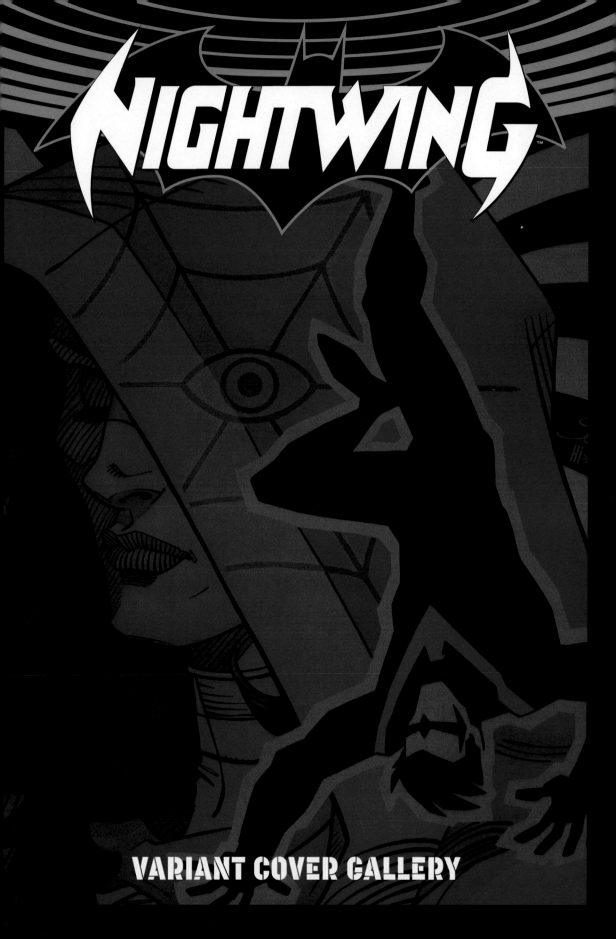

NIGHTWING #22 variant cover by CASEY JONES and HI-FI

NIGHTWING #26 variant cover by CASEY JONES and HI-FI

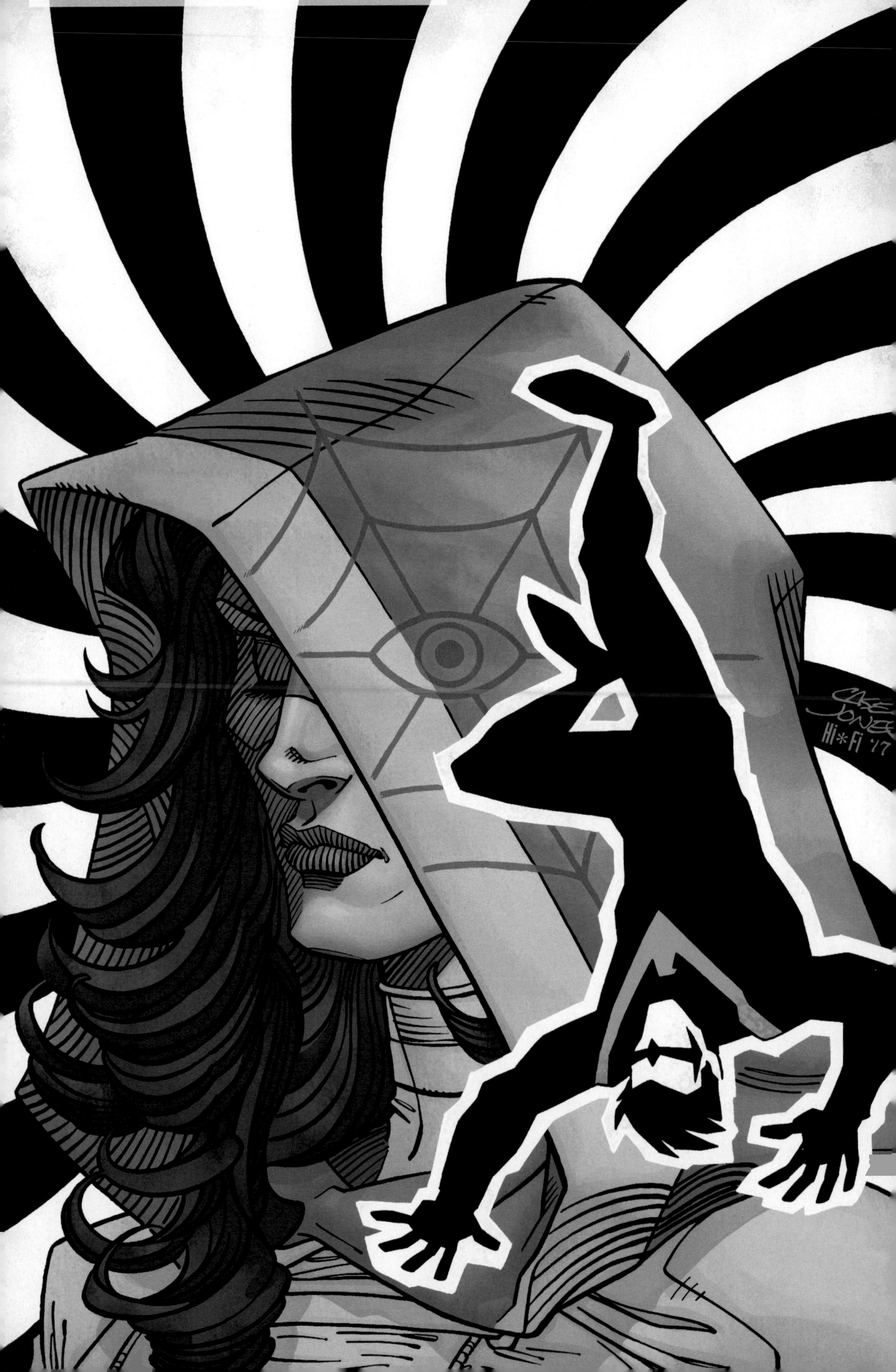

NIGHTWING #27 variant cover by CASEY JONES and HI-FI